Canadian Daily Language Activities

— Grade 8 —

Written by Eleanor M. Summers

Our Canadian Daily Language Activities series provides short and quick opportunities for students to review and reinforce skills in punctuation, grammar, spelling, language and reading comprehension. The Bonus Activities that follow each week of skills are fun tasks such as word and vocabulary puzzles, figurative language and reading exercises. A short interesting fact about Canada is the finishing touch!

ELEANOR M. SUMMERS is a retired teacher who is still actively involved in education. She has created many resources in language, science and history. As a writer, she enjoys creating practical and thought-provoking resources for teachers and parents.

Copyright © On The Mark Press 2016

This publication may be reproduced under licence from Access Copyright, or with the express written permission of On The Mark Press, or as permitted by law. All rights are otherwise reserved, and no part of this publication may be reproduced, stored in a retrieval system, or transmitted in any form or by any means, electronic, mechanical, photocopying, scanning, recording or otherwise, except as specifically authorized.

All Rights Reserved.
Printed in Canada.

Published in Canada by:
On The Mark Press
15 Dairy Avenue, Napanee, Ontario, K7R 1M4
www.onthemarkpress.com

Funded by the Government of Canada

#OTM2151

Topics cover:
Fluids and Dynamics, Systems in Action, and Light and Optical Systems.

#OTM2159

Topics cover:
The Planet Earth, Earth's Crust and Resources, and Heat in the Environment.

Master the Facts is a Hi/Lo Series developed to make history accessible to students at multiple skill levels and with various learning styles. Content is presented in a clear, concise manner for struggling learners with inquiry and application activities for students reading at grade level. There are two levels of questions for each topic. Illustrations, maps and diagrams visually enhance each topic and provide support for visual learners. 48 Master the Facts game cards review content learned.

#J199

#J1100

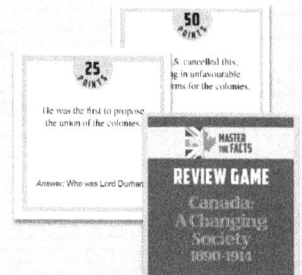

HOW TO USE: CANADIAN DAILY LANGUAGE ACTIVITIES

This book is divided into 32 weekly sections.

Each weekly section provides daily skill review and assessment activities.

ACTIVITIES 1 – 4

Focus is on:

- punctuation, capitalization, grammar, and spelling
- language and reading comprehension skills

ACTIVITY 5

Focus is on:

- a single language or reading skill

BONUS ACTIVITY

Provides opportunities for extended activities.

- word puzzles, vocabulary development
- spelling
- reading skills
- includes a short, interesting fact about Canada

STUDENT PROGRESS CHART

- Students record their daily score for each Language Activity.
- At the end of the week, they calculate their Total Score
- At the end of four weeks, students evaluate their performance.
- Students will require one copy of page 3 and three copies of page 4 to record results for entire 32 weeks. Teachers may wish to make back-to-back copies.

TEACHER SUGGESTIONS

- All activities may be completed for each week or teachers may exclude some.
- New skills may be completed as a whole class activity.
- Bonus Activities may be used at teachers' discretion.
- Correcting student work together will help model the correct responses.
- Monitor student mastery of skills from information on the Student Progress Chart.

_____'S PROGRESS CHART

How many did you get correct each day? Record your score on the chart.

Week	Activity 1	Activity 2	Activity 3	Activity 4	Activity 5	Total Score
#	/5	/5	/5	/5	/5	/25

Week	Activity 1	Activity 2	Activity 3	Activity 4	Activity 5	Total Score
#	/5	/5	/5	/5	/5	/25

Week	Activity 1	Activity 2	Activity 3	Activity 4	Activity 5	Total Score
#	/5	/5	/5	/5	/5	/25

Week	Activity 1	Activity 2	Activity 3	Activity 4	Activity 5	Total Score
#	/5	/5	/5	/5	/5	/25

My strongest skills are _____

My skills that need improvement are _____

The Bonus Activities I liked best are _____

Week	Activity 1	Activity 2	Activity 3	Activity 4	Activity 5	Total Score
#	/5	/5	/5	/5	/5	/25

Week	Activity 1	Activity 2	Activity 3	Activity 4	Activity 5	Total Score
#	/5	/5	/5	/5	/5	/25

Week	Activity 1	Activity 2	Activity 3	Activity 4	Activity 5	Total Score
#	/5	/5	/5	/5	/5	/25

Week	Activity 1	Activity 2	Activity 3	Activity 4	Activity 5	Total Score
#	/5	/5	/5	/5	/5	/25

My strongest skills are _____

My skills that need improvement are _____

The Bonus Activities I liked best are _____

_____'S PROGRESS CHART

How many did you get correct each day? Record your score on the chart.

Week	Activity 1	Activity 2	Activity 3	Activity 4	Activity 5	Total Score
#	/5	/5	/5	/5	/5	/25

Week	Activity 1	Activity 2	Activity 3	Activity 4	Activity 5	Total Score
#	/5	/5	/5	/5	/5	/25

Week	Activity 1	Activity 2	Activity 3	Activity 4	Activity 5	Total Score
#	/5	/5	/5	/5	/5	/25

Week	Activity 1	Activity 2	Activity 3	Activity 4	Activity 5	Total Score
#	/5	/5	/5	/5	/5	/25

My strongest skills are _____

My skills that need improvement are _____

The Bonus Activities I liked best are _____

Week	Activity 1	Activity 2	Activity 3	Activity 4	Activity 5	Total Score
#	/5	/5	/5	/5	/5	/25

Week	Activity 1	Activity 2	Activity 3	Activity 4	Activity 5	Total Score
#	/5	/5	/5	/5	/5	/25

Week	Activity 1	Activity 2	Activity 3	Activity 4	Activity 5	Total Score
#	/5	/5	/5	/5	/5	/25

Week	Activity 1	Activity 2	Activity 3	Activity 4	Activity 5	Total Score
#	/5	/5	/5	/5	/5	/25

My strongest skills are _____

My skills that need improvement are _____

The Bonus Activities I liked best are _____

DAILY LANGUAGE ACTIVITIES SKILLS LIST

This book provides many opportunities for practice of the following skills:

VOCABULARY & WORD SKILLS
- word meaning from context
- root words/prefixes/suffixes
- spelling
- syllabication
- synonyms/antonyms/homonyms
- contractions

CAPITALIZATION
- beginning of sentences
- proper names/titles of people
- names of places
- titles of books, songs, poems
- names of days, months, holidays
- abbreviations, initials

PUNCTUATION
- punctuation at the end of a sentence
- commas in a series
- commas in dates and addresses
- commas in compound and complex sentences
- commas after an introductory phrase/clause
- commas in direct address/parenthetical expressions
- commas after appositives
- commas between adjectives
- periods in abbreviations/initials
- punctuation & capitalization in simple dialogue
- use of colons, semicolons, dashes, parentheses
- quotation marks in speech
- quotation marks: poems, songs, stories
- apostrophes in contractions
- apostrophes in possessives
- interjections
- punctuation in friendly & business letters
- run on sentences
- underlining: books, plays, poems, magazines

GRAMMAR & WORD USAGE
- pronouns: subject/object, possessive
- pronoun antecedent
- singular/plural nouns
- nouns: abstract, concrete
- possessive nouns
- verb tenses, verb types, verb parts
- active & passive voice
- double negatives
- types of adjectives and adverbs
- correct form of adjective and adverbs
- correct article/determiner/adjective/adverb
- comparative/superlative forms
- predicate adjective; predicate nouns
- subject/predicate
- subject – verb agreement
- prepositional phrases; prepositions; objects of prepositions
- conjunctions
- phrases & clauses
- easily confused words
- sentence parts
- sentence types
- sentence structure
- sentence fragments
- sentence combinations

READING COMPREHENSION
- analogies
- figurative language
- inference
- idioms, proverbs

REFERENCE SKILLS
- combined errors
- dictionary/thesaurus skills
- outlines
- summaries

Name: _____

WEEK 1 — ACTIVITY 1 — TOTAL /5

Correct these sentences.

1. hey look at these its a canadian pennys witch we not longer us
   _____

2. hour coynes is the loony twoony quartar dime and nickle
   _____

Circle the *object* of the underlined preposition.

3. Rosi put her quarter <u>into</u> the machine but she didn't get a gumball.

4. A fierce wind blew the snow <u>over</u> the highway.

Write a contraction for the underlined words.

5. Our uncle <u>Paul is</u> coming to visit.   _____

Name: _____

WEEK 1 — ACTIVITY 2 — TOTAL /5

Underline the main verbs in this sentence.

1. The puppy jumped up on the bed, grabbed my library book and began to chew.

Correct these sentences.

2. eva were fasinated bye the grase and poise of the ballarina in the nutcracker
   _____

3. she went to the evning performance at the grand theater in hamilton
   _____

Write the plural form of each noun.

4. studio   _____

5. nucleus   _____

Name: _____

Complete each analogy.

1. Three is to triangle as eight is to _____

2. Carpet is to floor as bedspread is to _____

Correct these sentences.

3. there famly have a big orcherd with meny varietys of apples
   _____

4. thay make delisious sider by choping and pressing frash apples
   _____

Is the following text a *complete* sentence or a *fragment*?

5. Knowing you as well as I do.   _____

WEEK 1
ACTIVITY 3
TOTAL /5

Name: _____

Circle the *object* of the underlined preposition.

1. We didn't leave our house <u>during</u> the blizzard.

2. Mom got her car stuck <u>in</u> our driveway.

Correct these sentences.

3. we all agred that maxwell downes are the thoughfulest boy in hour class
   _____

4. mrs costini is opening a knew flour shop called blossom on fourth avenue
   _____

Circle the *indefinite pronoun* in this sentence.

5. Jake asked, "Does anyone know if we have math homework tonight?"

WEEK 1
ACTIVITY 4
TOTAL /5

Name: _____

Correct the errors in this business letter. Write each underlined part correctly.

(1) Setember 24 2015

(2) dear ms greenlees

(3) i wood like to invite you to our **(4)** next monthly meeting Please let me know if you can come.

(5) very truely yours

James Madison, Human Resources, KIMCO

1. _____
2. _____
3. _____
4. _____
5. _____

WEEK 1

ACTIVITY 5

TOTAL /5

Name: _____

Bonus Activity: What Happened Next?

When you write about something happening or something you do, it must be in the right time order. Another name for this is *chronology*.
Number these events in chronological order.

____ snap on the leash   ____ find an old Hallowe'en mask

____ bring your dog back home   ____ clean up your room

____ get the leash   ____ sneak up on your sister

____ whistle for your dog   ____ put it on

____ walk your dog   ____ jump out at her

WEEK 1

Arthur Sicard of Montreal, Quebec invented the first snowblower. He sold his first working prototype to the town of Outremont in 1927. He got the idea from watching a thresher harvest wheat in the fields. His neighbours thought his idea was crazy but he persisted. Today many Canadians are grateful that he did! **MY CANADA**

Name: _____

Correct these sentences.

1. last nite carrie fergot her ticket to the show lizzy fergot hers two

   _____

2. tokyo the capitol of japan is a hug city with milions of peple

   _____

Underline the *prepositions* in each sentence.

3. The play about a talking dog entertained everyone at the assembly on Friday.

4. Workers are working on the roof of the house next door.

Circle the *subject* and underline the *predicate*.

5. The boys in my class are organizing a football team.

WEEK 2
ACTIVITY 1
TOTAL /5

Name: _____

Underline the *predicate adjectives* in this sentence.

1. The glass of lemonade looked cold, delicious and inviting.

Circle the *linking verb* in each sentence.

2. When my mother makes cookies, the kitchen smells like chocolate.

3. Modern life has become complicated for many people.

Correct these sentences.

4. my cusins lives on a ranche in alberta they is vary lucky

   _____

5. we eight waffles with strawberrys syrip and whipped creem for brekfast

   _____

WEEK 2
ACTIVITY 2
TOTAL /5

Name: _____

WEEK 2 — ACTIVITY 3 — TOTAL /5

Underline the *subject* of this sentence.

1. A portrait of Sir John A. Macdonald is on our $10 bill.

Correct these sentences.

2. after he saw my fone bill dad exclaimed we gots to spend lesser muney
   _____

3. on twosday we gots to cetch the 7:30 bus if we wants to git to school erly
   _____

Are the underlined verbs *transitive* or *intransitive*?

4. Tourists <u>come</u> from all over the world to Niagara Falls.

5. Charlie <u>washed</u> the windows on the garden shed.

Name: _____

WEEK 2 — ACTIVITY 4 — TOTAL /5

Correct these sentences.

1. we has less players on are teem than them has on theres whined davie
   _____

2. there were a old twisted grape vin climbing the side of eddys barn
   _____

Complete these sentences with *who, which* or *what*.

3. Jackson, _____ is my cousin, will be the captain of our team.

4. Halifax, _____ is a big harbour, is the capital of Nova Scotia.

Is this sentence *declarative, interrogative, imperative,* or *exclamatory*?

5. Water the plants while I am away. _____

Name: _____

A *compound predicate* is made up of two or more verbs. Underline the verbs in each sentence.

WEEK 2

ACTIVITY 5

TOTAL /5

1. The waves splashed and pounded on the seawall.

2. The little child took a bath and went to bed.

3. The baby smiled and laughed at the teddy bear.

4. My dog runs and jumps and plays in the park.

5. The students finished their work and corrected it before the lunch break.

Name: _____

Bonus Activity: Context Clues

WEEK 2

A context clue is a hint from a sentence that helps you to figure out words you don't know. **Read each sentence. Write a definition of each underlined word.**

1. Dinosaurs were the <u>dominant</u> land animal millions of years ago.

   Meaning: _____

2. These animals reached <u>gigantic</u> proportions.

   Meaning: _____

3. Earlier and more <u>primitive</u> types were actually small, reptile-like animals.

   Meaning: _____

4. Suddenly all record of the giant animals stopped and they seemed to be <u>extinct</u>.

   Meaning: _____

> In 1888, a summer resort village was established at Lake Minniwanka. In 1941, a dam was built that raised the water level 30 meters (98 feet) totally submerging the village. Now scuba divers visit this glacier lake to explore the site of the submerged town.
>
> **MY CANADA**

Name: _____

WEEK 3 — ACTIVITY 1 — TOTAL /5

Correct these sentences.

1. josh dylan and emmet forgotten to tell theyre parents they kneaded a ride hoam

    _____

2. sallys aunt and unckle lives in ottawa and works on parliament hill

    _____

Circle the *antecedent* of the underlined pronouns.

3. Raw carrots are delicious and <u>they</u> are good for you.

4. Joan of Arc led troops into battle and <u>she</u> was victorious.

Is the underlined verb *transitive* or *intransitive*?

5. The company <u>named</u> a new CEO effective immediately.

Name: _____

WEEK 3 — ACTIVITY 2 — TOTAL /5

Underline the *prepositional phrase* in each sentence.

1. I always fall asleep under that warm, fuzzy blanket

2. Ella got a bad burn from the hot handle of the pot.

Correct these sentences.

3. wen i graderate frum hi school i plan to go to collage

    _____

4. seeings as how you is a good student im shure youll has no problum

    _____

Underline the *independent clause* in this sentence.

5. When I returned to the classroom, Ms. Watson had already left.

Name: _____

Write the correct form of the *adjective* to fit into each sentence.

1. Sophie is the _____ friend that I have. (kind)
2. Little Ryan is _____ than his brother. (noisy)

Correct these sentences.

3. althow him searched all over for hims books he couldnt find none of them
   _____

4. at the request of the principle the stewdents agreed to sergest ideas for fundrasing
   _____

Underline the *direct object* and circle the *indirect object* in this sentence.

5. I sent Barbara a postcard from Vancouver.

WEEK 3
ACTIVITY 3
TOTAL /5

Name: _____

Underline the *subordinate clause* in each sentence.

1. When the cold weather arrives, I hunt for my mitts.
2. If you know where they are, please tell me.

Correct these sentences.

3. ruth were so hungry she eight fore hame sandwitches fer lunch
   _____

4. besides hame she putted lettus musterd and pickels on each won
   _____

Complete this sentence with *who*, *which* or *what*.

5. Pauline Johnson is the poet _____ wrote "Prairie Greyhounds".

WEEK 3
ACTIVITY 4
TOTAL /5

Name: _____

Read the following paragraph and decide whether each underlined part has an error. Write *capitalization* **error,** *punctuation* **error,** *spelling* **error or** *no error.*

WEEK 3
ACTIVITY 5
TOTAL /5

(1)<u>joseph brant</u> belonged to the Mohawk tribe. As a boy, he attended a British school and was *(2)*<u>wall</u> educated. He became a leader *(3)*<u>among the Mohawks working to protect</u> their lands. Brant travelled *(4)*<u>through Iroquois lands</u> as well. He urged his people to fight against the *(5)*<u>americans</u>.

1. _____
2. _____
3. _____
4. _____
5. _____

Name: _____

Bonus Activity: Idioms

WEEK 3

Idioms are expressions with meanings different from the literal ones. **Explain the meaning of these idioms.**

1. Dinner is on the house tonight.
   _____

2. Janie got up on the wrong side of the bed. _____

3. I really am in the dark about what is going on. _____

4. Money burns a hole in my pocket.
   _____

5. He should mend fences before leaving.
   _____

6. Callie didn't have the hang of it yet.
   _____

In 2004, when our mint introduced the *world's first coloured coin.* The Canadian quarter proudly displayed a bright red poppy. The poppy is Canada's flower of remembrance, paying respect to Canada's veterans and fallen soldiers. **MY CANADA**

Name: _____

Correct these sentences.

1. we is not ready too leave fore school yet but well be once we ate brekfast

   _____

2. at exactly 910 a.m. hour bell rings to tell us class will begun

   _____

Underline the *linking verb* in each sentence.

3. Because we were shovelling gravel, we became dirty.

4. Nicky felt sick after riding the roller coaster.

Is this sentence *declarative, imperative, interrogative,* or *exclamatory*?

5. Although Canada has a great deal of fresh water, conservation is crucial.

   _____

WEEK 4
ACTIVITY 1
TOTAL /5

Name: _____

Complete this analogy.

1. ring is to finger as bracelet is to _____

Underline the *abstract nouns* in this sentence.

2. Black lab dogs are known for their intelligence and loyalty.

Circle the *infinitive* in this sentence.

3. Mom will show us how to make a chocolate cake.

Correct these sentences.

4. the furst kayaks was developed by ancesters of the inuit many yers ago

   _____

5. thay had a framewerk of whalebone or driftwood and was completly covered with sealskins

   _____

WEEK 4
ACTIVITY 2
TOTAL /5

Name: _____

Circle the *antecedent* of the underlined words.

1. Dean burned <u>his</u> finger when he touched the hot dish.

2. The company will explain <u>its</u> proposal tomorrow.

Correct these sentences.

3. my sister reba is taken a trip to simon fraser university in british columbia
   _____

4. she wants to inroll in classes their fore the upcomin simester
   _____

Write the root (base) word for:

5. unprecedented _____

WEEK 4
ACTIVITY 3
TOTAL /5

Name: _____

Tell if these verbs are *transitive* or *intransitive*.

1. My brother <u>coughed</u> so much last night that he kept me awake.
   _____

2. Mom <u>gave</u> him some cough syrup to help stop his cough. _____

Correct these sentences.

3. altho grandpa don't have no formal training he can build allmost enything
   _____

4. he builded a set of table and chairs for me and a hi chair for my brother stevie
   _____

Explain the meaning of the underlined figure of speech.

5. "<u>You've grown a foot</u>," exclaimed Aunt Gertie.
   _____

WEEK 4
ACTIVITY 4
TOTAL /5

Name: _____

Rewrite the following sentences to correctly punctuate the dialogue.

WEEK 4

ACTIVITY 5

TOTAL /5

1. I'll pick you up at three o'clock sharp said Mom so be ready
   _____

2. That's fine with me I replied I'll be waiting on the front step
   _____

3. Where are you going asked Jeff can I go with you and Mom
   _____

4. Not this time I answered my little brother we are going to the dentist
   _____

5. You're right Jeff exclaimed I will go with you some other time
   _____

Name: _____

Bonus Activity: Oxymoron

WEEK 4

An oxymoron is a two- or three- word phrase that contains opposite words or phrases. *Example:* a wise fool. **Explain in your own words:**

working vacation _____

definite maybe _____

Match the words in the box to create a common oxymoron.

		estimate
1. icy _____	4. bitter _____	memory
		hot
2. completely _____	5. exact _____	shrimp
		sweet
3. jumbo _____	6. forgettable _____	unfinished

MY CANADA

McAdam is a quiet, tiny town in southwestern New Brunswick. In the spring of 2012, it experienced a phenomenon called an "earthquake swarm". A series of 35 minor tremors struck the town over a five-week period, rattling windows and shaking floors.

Name: _____

Circle the *adverb* in this sentence. Does it tell *how, when, where* or to *what extent*?

1. David almost won the marathon race. _____

Correct these sentences.

2. i is haveing truble with sum of them there words said george

_____

3. has you looked in that there dicshunery or thesorus repiled ms bell

_____

Underline the subordinate clause in each sentence.

4. After we wash the dishes, we will put them away.

5. We went into the movie just as it was starting.

WEEK 5
ACTIVITY 1
TOTAL /5

Name: _____

Underline the *independent clause* in each sentence.

1. Whenever I hear that song, I want to dance.

2. We will help you as long as you co-operate with us.

Correct these sentences.

3. mom said dont be late for diner tonite i have a meating at the libary

_____

4. thay isn't goin nowhere on th weakend becus thay gots to werk

_____

Number these words to show their alphabetical order.

5. ____ mettle   ____ method   ____ meander   ____ medley   ____ metric

WEEK 5
ACTIVITY 2
TOTAL /5

Name: _____

Underline the *subject pronoun* and circle the *predicate pronoun* in each sentence.

1. The light was so bright it blinded us.

2. They will pay you for all of your hard work.

Circle the *simple subject* in this sentence.

3. Many kinds of birds can be found in that region of Canada.

Correct these sentences.

4. the campfir casted danceing shadoes on them people sitting neerby
   _____

5. we is gonna make a snak called smores from toasted marshmellows wafers and chocklit
   _____

WEEK 5
ACTIVITY 3
TOTAL /5

Name: _____

Write the meaning of this idiom.

1. <u>Quick as a flash</u>, the chipmunk was gone. _____

Correct these sentences.

2. the gam of trivia are a canadian invenshun its lottsa fun
   _____

3. you gots to have a good memery and no lottsa infermation
   _____

Are these nouns *singular* or *plural*?

4. oats   _____

5. umiak   _____

WEEK 5
ACTIVITY 4
TOTAL /5

Name: _____

Combine these sentences to make one good sentence.

WEEK 5
ACTIVITY 5
TOTAL /5

1. Jack wanted to go camping with us. He got sick. He couldn't go.
   _____

2. Our sump pump stopped working. Our basement flooded. It was a huge mess.
   _____

3. Toronto is one of the biggest cities in Canada. It used to be called York.
   _____

4. A small, white kitten came to our door. It had no collar. We will try to find the owner.
   _____

5. Everyone was watching the World Series. It was the final game. It was exciting.
   _____

Name: _____

Bonus Activity: Concrete or Abstract?

WEEK 5

A *concrete noun* is something you can see, hear, touch, smell or taste. An *abstract noun* is something you may not be able to see – an idea, a feeling, or a quality – but you know that it exists.

Read the story below. Circle the *concrete nouns in red* and the *abstract nouns in blue*.

A student in my class wrote a story about unusual courage. It told of a group of soldiers fighting in a foreign land. We value personal freedom in Canada and their bravery helped us to keep it. When they returned to their own country, they were honoured with a parade and presented with medals of valour. We should remain loyal to these citizens who fought to gain peace and freedom.

In 2012, a robbery was discovered at the Global Strategic Syrup Reserve in Quebec. Six million pounds of syrup, or $18 million dollars worth was stolen. Sticky-fingered thieves, eh?

MY CANADA

Name: _____

WEEK 6 — ACTIVITY 1

Correct these sentences.

1. my fotos of hour vacashun turned out more better than me expected
   _____

2. leo and lena my cousuns has invited us to go to the sircus with thems
   _____

TOTAL /5

Circle the *direct object* and underline the *indirect object* in each sentence.

3. They have opened an animal rescue centre for abandoned pets.

4. They provide food, shelter and medical care for all the animals

Underline the helping, or *auxiliary*, verbs in this sentence.

5. We did not have enough money for a treat, so we had to wait until another time.

Name: _____

WEEK 6 — ACTIVITY 2

How many syllables does each word have?

1. accordingly _____   pemmican _____

Underline the *indefinite pronoun* in each sentence.

2. We thought we heard something scratching on our window pane.

3. It was nothing more than a tree branch.

TOTAL /5

Correct these sentences.

4. carrits is a heathful vegetable some people ownly ate them raw
   _____

5. im shure well see lottsa people we knew at the annaversary party on sunday
   _____

Name: _____

WEEK 6 — ACTIVITY 3 — TOTAL /5

Write the meaning of the underlined idiom.

1. The sick child wasn't <u>out of the woods yet</u>.

   _____

Underline the *infinitives* in each sentence.

2. I hope to travel to Ireland to meet some of my relatives.

3. You need to feed the dog and to bath it.

Correct these sentences.

4. in 1534 the king of france sended jacques cartier to north amarica

   _____

5. hims task were to serch for gold and preshus medals then clame the land fore franc

   _____

Name: _____

WEEK 6 — ACTIVITY 4 — TOTAL /5

Correct these sentences.

1. meny setlers comed over to canada on crouded saling ships

   _____

2. there jurney were filled with dangers sich as storms lacke of food and diseaze

   _____

Underline the *coordinating conjunctions* in each sentence.

3. You may either go to a movie or invite a friend over for dinner.

4. Not only is Darren a skillful athlete but he also is a good student.

Underline the *past participle* in this sentence.

5. Sharon hates getting to school after the bell rings.

Name: _____

Rewrite this short paragraph, correcting all the punctuation errors.

thursday december 6 1917 was a bright clear day in halifax nova scotia for some reason two ships the mont blanc a munitions carrier and the norwegian steamer imo steered for the same side of the narrow channel joining halifax harbour and bedford basin when the ships collided a fire ignited the munitions ship the explosion blew the mont blanc to pieces and heaved the imo onto the dartmouth shore on that disastrous day 2000 people were killed and 9000 were injured this became known as the halifax explosion

WEEK 6
ACTIVITY 5
TOTAL /5

___
___
___
___
___
___
___
___

Name: _____

Bonus Activity: Canadian, Eh?

Complete the chart by naming three items that fit the category and that are Canadian.

WEEK 6

Category	Item 1	Item 2	Item 3
A sports team			
A piece of clothing			
A bird			
An animal			
A special food			
A tourist attraction			

MY CANADA The *wood frog* of British Columbia and the Maritimes has a rare survival skill for our brutal winters. When the temperature reaches from -1° and -6° Celsius, they become frog ice cubes or .... frogsicles! They hibernate underground so when the soil freezes, so do the frogs.

Name: _____

WEEK 7 — ACTIVITY 1 — TOTAL /5

Correct these sentences.

1. them beutiful silver earings was a gift frum my grandmother irene

_____

2. she weared thum fifty years ago on her weding day

_____

Underline the *correlative conjunctions* in these sentences.

3. Neither Jill nor her sister are willing to help us.

4. Whether you believe me or not, that story is true.

Underline the *direct object* and circle the *indirect object* in this sentence.

5. Somebody left you a message.

Name: _____

WEEK 7 — ACTIVITY 2 — TOTAL /5

Underline the *infinitives* in each sentence

1. Do you think students should be forced to wear school uniforms?

2. Wouldn't it be expensive to buy them?

Underline the *prepositional phrase* in this sentence.

3. There has been a great deal of flooding in our community.

Correct these sentences.

4. sid the kid is a nikname for nhl hockey player sidney crosby

_____

5. the more exsiting time of my live was goin to a one direction rock consert

_____

Name: _____

WEEK 7

ACTIVITY 3

Write the *subject* of this sentence.

1. When using a sharp knife, be careful not to cut yourself. _____

Correct these sentences.

2. the girl swum acrost the pool and back at leest ate times
   _____

3. my grandpa harry are kinde generus and my bestest freind said louis
   _____

Circle the *antecedent* for each underlined pronoun.

4. The boy played baseball with <u>his</u> friends.

5. Marnie and Frank rode <u>their</u> bikes to school.

TOTAL /5

Name: _____

WEEK 7

ACTIVITY 4

Correct these sentences.

1. fog cuvered the areport preventing sevral plains frum landing
   _____

2. did the magican poll a bowkay of flours from under a skarf asked billy
   _____

Complete this analogy.

3. Ghost is to Hallowe'en as bunny is to _____.

Underline the *indefinite pronoun*.

4. Several kids in my math class are having trouble with the work.

5. A few of us are going to form a peer tutor group to help them.

TOTAL /5

Name: _____

WEEK 7

ACTIVITY 5

TOTAL /5

Read the following paragraph. Explain the meaning of the underlined words.

Bart sat sullenly against the cement wall, waiting. Soon they would come for him. If they thought this waiting *(1)could loosen his tongue* and make him *(2)squeal on his buddies*, they were wrong. Either way he was a *(3)dead duck* and soon it would be over. He had been caught *(4)like a rat in a trap* and it had been his fault. He faced the firing squad *(5)like a solitary wolf*, alone but not afraid.

1. _____

2. _____

3. _____

4. _____

5. _____

Name: _____

WEEK 7

Bonus Activity: Tone

The *tone* of a story or sentence is the feeling it has and the feeling it makes the reader have. Some examples of tone are: happy, fearful, excited, frantic, wishful. **Write the tone set by each sentence.**

1. I can't believe the history test is today. I forgot to study. _____

2. My best friend Polly is moving away. I am really going to miss her. _____

3. Today is my birthday! I know it will be a great day. _____

4. The sun is shining and the air smells fresh. It feels good to be alive!
_____

5. The fans went wild when the home team scored. _____

MY CANADA

Every year between April and June, a new crop of icebergs, beginning as pieces broken from Greenland glaciers, float by the coasts of Labrador and Newfoundland. While about 40,000 icebergs break off in Greenland, only 500 – 800 make as far as St. John's, Newfoundland.

Name: _____

Correct these sentences.

1. erly explores wundered if their relly were a northwest passage around north america

   _____

2. by 1845 most sailers new that any passage wood be locked in ise most of the year

   _____

Are these sentences *simple*, *compound* or *complex*?

3. That story was a great mystery!   _____

4. When the main character got lost, I held my breath. _____

Underline the *abstract nouns* in this sentence.

5. Mom's best qualities are her patience and her cheerfulness.

WEEK 8
ACTIVITY 1
TOTAL /5

Name: _____

Circle the *coordinating conjunction* in each sentence.

1. You will pass the test if you have studied for it.

2. Hank tried to hit the target but missed every time.

How many syllables in this word?

3. penitentiary   _____

Correct these sentences.

4. jane werks dalivering pizza she makes 2500 evry nite

   _____

5. hour sckool have a junior authers club i hope to joyne

   _____

WEEK 8
ACTIVITY 2
TOTAL /5

Name: _____

Are the following texts a complete sentence or fragment?

1. It is helpful to know how to read a map. _____

2. Easy to get lost. _____

Correct these sentences.

3. lynn and me is allways arguing about whose the best socker player
_____

4. if you really doesnt want a berthday presant i well donate to a cherity
_____

Underline the *prepositions* in this sentence. Then circle the *objects of the prepositions*.

5. Let's follow the path into the field, along the river and into the woods.

WEEK 8
ACTIVITY 3
TOTAL /5

Name: _____

Correct these sentences.

1. reeding, is hour favorit weigh to spend a reiny and cold afternoon
_____

2. if you doesnt want to reed we can play sum bored games
_____

Circle the *antecedent* of the underlined pronoun.

3. Brad gave all the little kids a ride in <u>his</u> wagon.

Underline the *subordinate clause* in each sentence.

4. I am returning this book because I have finished reading it.

5. You heard me calling you yet you did not answer me.

WEEK 8
ACTIVITY 4
TOTAL /5

Name: _____

Combine the following sentences to make one good sentence.

1. Mom cooked pancakes. We ate them for breakfast. They were delicious!
   _____

2. Peter went to college. He went in September. He is studying to be a vet tech.
   _____

3. The car came to a halt. The battery went dead. It will need to be towed.
   _____

4. I will start to make a cake. I need to gather the ingredients. I need to read the directions.
   _____

5. Dad had a sore back. He raked leaves all day Saturday. He is going to the doctor.
   _____

WEEK 8
ACTIVITY 5
TOTAL /5

Name: _____

Bonus Activity: Words! Words! Words!

Fill in the blanks with a word (or words) that mean the same as the one in brackets. Use a dictionary or a thesaurus if you need help.

Archaeologists worked for months in the _____ (dark, damp) cave. They were trying to _____ (decipher) the ancient code on the rock walls. The rough walls made it _____ (very hard) to see the markings. The carvings were barely _____ (legible) even to the trained eye. Legend says some explorers had strangely _____ (disappeared) inside the cave. Sometimes _____ (audible) moans could be heard in the distance. Do you believe such a thing is _____? (true)

WEEK 8

MY CANADA

Canada's Wonderland is the nation's largest amusement park and one of the biggest in North America. Opened on May 23, 1981, it boasts more that 200 attractions, 69 rides, a water park and live shows.

Name: _____

Are these sentences *simple*, *compound*, or *complex*?

1. We like to run fast and jump in a big pile of leaves. _____

2. We will understand the facts if we listen carefully. _____

Correct these sentences.

3. coffee tee and hot chocklit is served for brekfast in the dinner
_____

4. my sister savannah gots a pear of fuzzy pyjamas fore her berthday
_____

Circle the *simple subject* and underline the *simple predicate*.

5. The boy riding the bicycle is my brother.

WEEK 9
ACTIVITY 1
TOTAL /5

Name: _____

Circle the *conjunction* in each sentence.

1. Because they were so hungry, the boys gobbled their food.

2. We will be drawing names and buying gifts at Boys and Girls' Club.

Underline the *prepositional phrases* in this sentence.

3. I was late for the bus, so I grabbed an apple for a snack and a cookie for a treat.

Correct these sentences.

4. a farmer livin along the niagara river in the 1700s sold a cow to an american farmer
_____

5. but the homesick cow swum back to her canadian owner and would not life elsewear
_____

WEEK 9
ACTIVITY 2
TOTAL /5

Name: _____

Is the underlined verb *transitive* or *intransitive*?

WEEK **9**

1. The rookie scored the winning goal. _____

Correct these sentences.

ACTIVITY **3**

2. dering a electricul storm the power may fall and bee off for hours

_____

TOTAL **/5**

3. my most old sister karen were born on june 19 2000 in hamilton ontario

_____

Underline the *adverb* in each sentence. Does it tell *how, where, when,* or to *what extent*?

4. She generously gave everyone a share of her treats. _____

5. Lately you seem very tired. _____

Name: _____

Correct these sentences.

WEEK **9**

1. can you plese give tara sum help loding the dishwasher asked martha

_____

ACTIVITY **4**

2. we love bergers and frys for our friday nite super

_____

Use context clues to explain the meaning of the underlined word sentence.

TOTAL **/5**

3. The locket I got for my birthday is <u>inscribed</u> with my initials.

_____

Underline the *linking verbs* in each sentence.

4. This cake smells good and tastes even better!

5. The soccer player was a superstar but appears very shy.

Name: _____

Read the following sentences and decide whether the underlined part has an error. Write *capitalization* **error,** *punctuation* **error,** *spelling* **error or** *no error*.

WEEK 9

ACTIVITY 5

TOTAL /5

1. <u>On Saturday Dad and I</u> went to a professional basketball game.
   _____

2. We <u>rode the crowded subway</u> to the game.
   _____

3. The <u>air canada centre</u> was more crowded than the subway.
   _____

4. We both wanted the <u>Toronto Rapters</u> to win.
   _____

5. It was a win for <u>the hometown team</u>?
   _____

Name: _____

Bonus Activity: What's the Effect?

WEEK 9

Whatever makes something happen is called the *cause*. **Read the causes below. Write a reasonable effect for each cause.**

Cause	Effect
1. losing your wallet	
2. watching eight hours of television	
3. eating too much candy	
4. oversleeping on a school morning	
5. forgetting to do your homework	
6. your dog running through the house	

There are no communities in Nunavut *that are accessible by road or railway. Everything, and everyone, arrives by air or water.*

MY CANADA

Name: _____

Circle the *participles* in these sentences.

WEEK 10
ACTIVITY 1

1. The crying baby kept us awake all night.

2. The howling winds whipped the snow into big drifts.

Correct these sentences.

3. sense they was sick we couldnt watch the world series togather

_____

4. whip youre derty boots befor youse come into my kitchin sadi aunt lucy

_____

Circle the prefix that means " across"

5. inter   post   trans   non

TOTAL /5

Name: _____

Underline the future perfect verb in each sentence.

WEEK 10
ACTIVITY 2

1. By the end of this week, I will have finished reading this book.

2. We shall elect a new leader of our student council.

Underline the *interrogative adjective* in this sentence.

3. What stores did you visit on your shopping trip?

Correct these sentences.

4. the son melted them there icicles that was hangin from the roofe

_____

5. julie cutted the watermelin into a dozin peaces fore us to ate

_____

TOTAL /5

Name: _____

WEEK 10
ACTIVITY 3
TOTAL /5

Underline the *abstract nouns* in this sentence.

1. Your story demonstrates imagination and insight.

Correct these sentences.

2. kellys hobbys include the following photography saling and hikeing
   _____

3. he taked a foto of a iceburg drifting off the shores of labradoor
   _____

Underline the *independent clause* in each sentence.

4. When we got to the theatre, it was noisy and crowded.

5. Jack put his bike in the garage so it wouldn't get wet in the rain.

Name: _____

WEEK 10
ACTIVITY 4
TOTAL /5

Rewrite these sentences to correct the run-ons.

1. Colin was invited to a party it was a birthday party it was his friend's birthday.
   _____

2. We went to the cafeteria we wanted to buy lunch we wanted a turkey wrap.
   _____

Correct these sentences.

3. they're isnt nothing you can dew about the whether exclaimed grandpa
   _____

4. cant no one in hour class solve this here puzzle asked fred
   _____

Write a good sentence to show the meaning of the word "temporary"

5. _____

Name: _____

A *restrictive clause* is a clause that is **necessary** to the meaning of a sentence. A *non-restrictive clause* is a clause that is **not necessary** to the meaning. A non-restrictive clause is set off from the rest of the sentence by commas.

Write R (restrictive) or NR (non-restrictive) for the underlined clauses. Add commas where needed.

WEEK 10

ACTIVITY 5

TOTAL /5

1. Sharon who is a very kind person tries to see the best in everyone. _____
2. Tarts are small pastry shells that contain delicious fillings. _____
3. The Beech Bay Campground where my family goes in summer is nearby. _____
4. The sun which was very hot today gave me a sunburn. _____
5. The school that I attended as a child is closing in June. _____

Name: _____

Bonus Activity: Analogies

WEEK 10

Solve the puzzle by completing the analogy for each clue. Write one letter in each box.

Clue: complete the analogy

1. paw is to dog as ____ is to fish						
2. writer is to story as poet is to ____						
3. bear is to ____ as bee is to hive						
4. ____ is to pool as jog is to road						
5. Bob is to Robert as Susie is to ____						
6. Edmonton is to Alberta as Montreal is to ____						

MY CANADA — The deadliest earthquake in Canadian history struck on Nov. 18, 1929. The 7.2 magnitude quake caused a tsunami on Newfoundland's Burin Peninsula, claiming 27 lives.

Name: _____

Correct these sentences.

1. frannies mom sowed every won of them there costumes for hour play

   _____

2. itsa long long bus ride from calgary to ottawa

   _____

Underline the *indefinite pronouns* in each sentence.

3. Anyone can play this game and nobody will object.

4. Somebody left something on our front step today.

Underline the *prepositional phrases*.

5. All students in the band will be going to the competition in April.

WEEK 11
ACTIVITY 1
TOTAL /5

Name: _____

Complete each sentence with the correct word.

1. Which cake tastes better, Martha's or _____?   **her / mine / your / me**

2. Jack's drawing looks a lot like _____ .   **he / she / yours / their**

Correct these sentences.

3. we is going on a vacasion to florida in the march brake

   _____

4. is you flying or driveing yore car asked pete

   _____

Is the following text a *fragment* or a *complete* sentence?

5. As soon as we get the message   _____

WEEK 11
ACTIVITY 2
TOTAL /5

Name: _____

Correct these sentences.

1. my favrit character in that there story is the hero princess ella

   _____

2. she were not afrade to defend her kingdum aganst the evel which

   _____

Underline the *participle*. **Circle the** *noun* **that the participle modifies**

3. Soft pattering rain could be heard on the barn roof.

4. Blowing snow and freezing rain made driving dangerous.

Use context to explain the meaning of the underlined word.

5. The game warden will be checking for lawbreakers in that park.

   _____

WEEK 11
ACTIVITY 3
TOTAL /5

Name: _____

Are these sentences *declarative, interrogative, imperative,* **or** *exclamatory*?

1. Do we have any chocolate-covered raisins for my snack? _____

2. Help shovel the snow from the driveway and sweep off the steps.
   _____

Correct these sentences.

3. when ever hour dog jedi see the school bus he jump up and down in won spot

   _____

4. i doesnt injoy doin the dishes but i knows that mom needs my halp

   _____

Underline the *infinitives* **in this sentence.**

5. If you want to succeed you will need to stay focused and to work hard.

WEEK 11
ACTIVITY 4
TOTAL /5

Name: _____

Rewrite the sentences to correct the run-ons.

WEEK **11**

ACTIVITY **5**

TOTAL /5

1. Bob didn't want to wash the car I didn't want to wash the car Mom made us do it anyway.
   _____

2. Fresh fruits are sold at market vegetables are sold there we bought some.
   _____

3. My pen and pencil fell they fell off my desk they fell onto the floor.
   _____

4. At the party Cory and Bill dressed up they were ghosts they scared the little kids.
   _____

5. The cheerleaders and fans yelled they cheered for the home team they were loud.
   _____

Name: _____

Bonus Activity: Keep It Short

WEEK **11**

Write the meaning of each abbreviation.

1. Jr. _____
2. ASAP _____
3. Aug. _____
4. max. _____
5. etc. _____

6. B.A. _____
7. c.o.d. _____
8. R.S.V.P. _____
9. cm _____
10. cont. _____

MY CANADA   *Bobby Hull* was the first hockey player to sign a million-dollar contract. He signed with the Winnipeg Jets on June 27, 1972. How does that compare with today's salaries?

SSR1151   ISBN: 9781771587471 © On The Mark Press

Name: _____

Underline the *adverbs* in this sentence.

1. Greg is often late, seldom prepared for class, and frequently tired.

Correct these sentences.

2. selma want to joyne the mystery readers book club but her are two bizzy write now
   _____

3. we meat each thursday at lincoln park library at 400 pm sharpe
   _____

Underline the *subject pronoun* and circle the *object pronoun* in each sentence.

4. Everyone needs to find their uniform and return it to the coach.

5. He would never allow it to be lost.

WEEK 12
ACTIVITY 1
TOTAL /5

Name: _____

Correct these sentences.

1. vitamuns found in froots and vegetabuls is vary good for yore health
   _____

2. wee spended alot of time practiceing our song fore the consert
   _____

Circle the *antecedent* of the underlined pronouns in these sentences.

3. The girls enjoyed that book so much that they read it twice.

4. Our dog barks at the mailman because it does not know him.

Write the contractions for these words.

5. she had _____   I will _____

WEEK 12
ACTIVITY 2
TOTAL /5

Name: _____

WEEK 12 — ACTIVITY 3

TOTAL /5

Correct these sentences.

1. watch out didnt you sea that broken step asked della
   _____

2. no i didnt della replyed thanks four warning me
   _____

Underline the subordinate clause in each sentence.

3. Finish your report before it gets too late.

4. As soon as we heard the news, we all cheered.

How many syllables does each word have?

5. reciprocal _____   horizontal _____

Name: _____

WEEK 12 — ACTIVITY 4

TOTAL /5

Correct these sentences.

1. if all gos well grandma norma will arrive from halifax on sunday
   _____

2. the book mystery of skull island are a reel thriller it mite skare you
   _____

Tell the *number* and *gender* of these nouns.

3. men   _____

4. niece   _____

Is the underlined verb *transitive* or *intransitive*?

5. The toddler <u>stamped</u> his feet on the floor.

Name: _____

Combine these sentences to make one good sentence.

1. Jimmy is learning to ride his bicycle. He needs to wear a helmet. He should pedal slowly.
   _____

2. Lucas and Tom are playing. They love to play baseball. They play it every day.
   _____

3. The movers came to our house. They loaded our furniture. They were careful.
   _____

4. My computer is broken. It will not turn on. I will need to get it repaired.
   _____

5. Alice wants a new doll. She wants a Baby Susie. She wants it for her birthday.
   _____

WEEK 12
ACTIVITY 5
TOTAL /5

Name: _____

Bonus Activity: Time for Action!

Underline all of the *verbs* and *verb phrases* in the following paragraph.
HINT: Try to find 25 answers.

This morning, I woke up late and jumped out of bed. I landed on my sister's stuffed dog, lost my balance, stumbled and fell. My sister Carrie came into my room, rubbed her eyes and demanded "Who is making all that noise?" I grumbled a few words and headed downstairs. Carrie walked slowly to her room and jumped back into bed. Mom heard the racket and came to see what was going on. "Why are you girls making so much noise on a Saturday morning?" she asked. "You woke up far too early." I nodded to show that I agreed with Mom, grabbed some toast and went back to my room so I could sleep some more.

WEEK 12

MY CANADA
The Quebec Winter Carnival is the largest winter carnival in the world. The first festival took place in 1894, but the present style event began in 1955.

Name: _____

Underline the *conjunction* in this sentence.

1. Until I hear from my sister, I will wait at home.

Correct these sentences.

2. the hole class injoyed the trip to the royal ontario museim last march

_____

3. every one have there favrit exhibut but mine were animul habitats

_____

Rewrite these phrases using a possessive noun.

4. the beautiful leaves of the maple tree _____

5. the excited fans of the final game _____

WEEK 13
ACTIVITY 1
TOTAL /5

Name: _____

Underline the *direct object* and circle the *indirect object* in this sentence.

1. The music teacher taught the choir a new song.

Use context to explain the meanings of the underlined words.

2. <u>Lichen</u> was growing everywhere on the rocks.

_____

3. He has been <u>estranged</u> from his son for many years.

_____

Correct these sentences.

4. the fans was leaveing becuz the game were doll and boaring

_____

5. you shouldnt made plans fore the wekend untell you ask yur parants

_____

WEEK 13
ACTIVITY 2
TOTAL /5

Name: _____

Underline the *adverb*. Does it tell how, where, when or to what extent?

1. You will have the answer to your question soon.

Correct these sentences.

2. after a big sno are a grate time to go toboganing skiing ore skidoing

   _____

3. ware warm close thicke mits yore helmut and rember to keep save

   _____

Underline the *participle*. Circle the *noun that the participle modifies*.

4. We noticed the inviting smell of popcorn as soon as we entered the theatre.

5. Blowing snow and lashing winds made driving difficult.

WEEK 13 — ACTIVITY 3 — TOTAL /5

Name: _____

Write a good sentence that shows the meaning for this word: emblem

1. _____

Correct these sentences.

2. cora uses brite colers in hers pitures but he sister hallie perfers pastal colers

   _____

3. is you lookin four yur reeding glasses i asked grandpa ralph

   _____

Circle the *antecedent* of the underlined pronoun in each sentence.

4. When settlers came to Canada, <u>they</u> had a difficult life.

5. The country was rich in resources but <u>it</u> was rugged and untamed.

WEEK 13 — ACTIVITY 4 — TOTAL /5

Name: _____

Read the following paragraph and decide if the underlined part has a *spelling* error, a *capitalization* error or a *punctuation* error. Write the correct form on the lines below.

WEEK **13**

ACTIVITY **5**

TOTAL **/5**

(1)<u>Long ago when a wise and brave chief died</u> people wanted to **(2)**<u>honor</u> him. They would pile stones into a cairn on a nearby hilltop. **(3)**<u>around the cairn</u> they laid out stones lines and circles. **(4)**<u>Many years afterwards</u> newcomers to the area found the stone circles. They called it **(5)**<u>medicine wheel</u>.

1. _____
2. _____
3. _____
4. _____
5. _____

Name: _____

Bonus Activity: All About Adjectives

WEEK **13**

Read each phrase and circle the *adjective*. Write the adjectives in the correct column to tell what they answer.

Phrase	What kind?	How many?	Which one?
1. old man			
2. three sisters			
3. this cookie			
4. yellow socks			
5. those flowers			

MY CANADA

McCain Foods is the world's largest manufacturer of French fries. One out of every three French fries eaten on Earth is a McCain fry. Their headquarters is located in Florenceville-Bristol, New Brunswick.

Name: _____

Correct these sentences.

1. linda showed lara her knew snobored her gots fore christmas
   _____

2. the instructer ofered to give her too free lessins dering the brake
   _____

Explain the meaning of the underlined word by using context clues.

3. The bank has a <u>lien</u> on his car until the debt is paid.
   _____

Underline the *coordinating conjunction* in each sentence.

4. You want to make the basketball team but you don't come to practice.

5. We will rehearse every day and the play will be a success.

WEEK **14**
ACTIVITY **1**
TOTAL /5

Name: _____

Correct these sentences.

1. in 1665 king lewis the xiv of france sended some mairs and stallions to new france
   _____

2. after a few yeers evry fermer in new france owned at lest won horse of there own
   _____

Circle the best word to complete the sentence.

3. I bought that bag of candy. It is _____ .   **theirs / ours / mine / hers**

4. Grandpa owns a vintage car. It is _____ .   **theirs / ours / mine / his**

Is this sentence *declarative, imperative, interrogative,* or *exclamatory*?

5. What is the best memory of your childhood? _____

WEEK **14**
ACTIVITY **2**
TOTAL /5

46

Name: _____

Underline helping, or *auxiliary*, verbs in these sentences.

1. Charlie was telling a story about hunting bears with his uncle.

2. Is he making it up or could it be true?

Correct these sentences.

3. well you driv me to basball practise mom i asked real polite
   _____

4. if you well halp me dew the dishs and cleen up the kitchin she replyed
   _____

Circle the *simple subject* of this sentence.

5. The foreign spy risked his life to save his partner.

WEEK 14
ACTIVITY 3
TOTAL /5

Name: _____

Correct these sentences.

1. wen we gots to the aerport in ottawa the plain had allready taked of
   _____

2. we had to wate their for ate ours until the next flite were ready to took off
   _____

Underline the *past perfect verb* in each sentence.

3. Sam had removed his muddy shoes at the door.

4. Earlier that day, his mom had placed a mat at the door for him.

Circle the *prefix* that means "after"

5. sub   con   post   mis

WEEK 14
ACTIVITY 4
TOTAL /5

Name: _____

Combine these sentences to make one good sentence.

1. The house was old. It looked run-down. The new owners have plans to renovate it.
   _____

2. The little boy was all alone. He looked cold and hungry. No one noticed him.
   _____

3. We went out for seafood dinner. We went to Specialty Seafoods. I had jumbo shrimp.
   _____

4. Have you seen Harry's painting? It is a seascape. It shows his grandparents' home.
   _____

5. Kent is very sick with strep throat. He didn't mention any signs of it. He didn't complain.
   _____

WEEK 14
ACTIVITY 5
TOTAL /5

Name: _____

Bonus Activity: Homophones

Words that sound the same often have very different meanings. **Circle the word that means the same as the first word.**

1. strength	might	mite
2. religious song	him	hymn
3. musical instrument	symbol	cymbal
4. well-liked	popular	poplar
5. French money	franc	frank
6. forbidden	band	banned

WEEK 14

"Cow-patty bingo" is a popular fund-raising event. 150 squares are drawn on a street or field; numbered and sold for $10 each. The cows arrive and if one "picks" your square, you will win a prize!

MY CANADA

Name: _____

WEEK 15 — ACTIVITY 1 — TOTAL /5

Underline the *independent clause* in each sentence.

1. Besides being a soccer player, Tony plays in the school band.

2. Andrea cleaned up her room although she complained about it.

Circle the *prepositional phrases* in this sentence.

3. The old dog was lying on the porch in the shade of the big oak tree

Correct these sentences.

4. sense yule bee late fore school isle give youse a ride this wunce

   _____

5. the fabels and lejends of a contry tell alot about there culture

   _____

Name: _____

WEEK 15 — ACTIVITY 2 — TOTAL /5

Underline the *complete subject* and circle the *simple subject*.

1. Greta, who is my best friend, visits her Grandma every Sunday.

Correct these sentences.

2. we want fishin for trout all we cot were a old boot and a rustee can

   _____

3. terry shell i fry boil or ovan roste yore catch joked dad

   _____

Write the plural form of each noun.

4. mother-in-law _____

5. avocado _____

Name: _____

Circle the *linking verb* in this sentence.

1. The task of raking all the leaves seemed impossible.

Tell if each sentence is *declarative, imperative, interrogative,* or *exclamatory*.

2. Do you have any honey doughnuts? _____

3. What a close call we had on the road today! _____

Correct these sentences.

4. stella keps a dairy she rights in it evry day about thing that has hapened

   _____

5. the last voyage of the scotian is a eksiting tail of advenchure on a ship

   _____

WEEK 15
ACTIVITY 3
TOTAL /5

Name: _____

Circle the *abstract nouns* in each sentence.

1. Many people today live in poverty and despair.

2. Your kindness and generosity will not be forgotten.

Correct these sentences.

3. ross loked away frum mr markams stirn glance and begun to werk

   _____

4. i is jest starting to read the dog that woodn't bee by farley mowat

   _____

Is the verb in this sentence *active* or *passive* voice?

5. Pauline was blamed for the gossip by her friends. _____

WEEK 15
ACTIVITY 4
TOTAL /5

Name: _____

WEEK 15

Commas are used to separate words in a series or to set off a person's name when that person is being spoken to. **Place commas correctly in these sentences.**

ACTIVITY 5

TOTAL /5

1. Casey's favourite subjects in school are math science art and sometimes history.

2. Tommy could you play with the new boy at recess today?

3. Mrs. Bennett would you like me to babysit after school tonight?

4. Amy wants to babysit walk dogs scoop ice cream or deliver papers for the summer.

5. Melanie you cannot borrow my bicycle ever again!

Name: _____

Bonus Activity: Story Board

WEEK 15

On the back, create a storyboard for the following short story. Illustrate each paragraph in one box on the storyboard. Use speech bubbles to retell the story.

1. One day, Sally and Dana were riding their bicycles along a country road. When they stopped to rest for a minute, they noticed something in the bushes.

2. "What's that?" Sally whispered. Dana looked more closely. "It's furry." she said

3. Both girls stood and stared into the bushes. Then, all of a sudden, they saw "it" move just a bit.

4. "That scared me," said Sally. "It's only a baby rabbit, "said Dana. "It is more afraid of us!"

MY CANADA

Saskatchewan is the largest producer of *mustard* in the world. An estimated 300,000 to 400,000 acres of land is *given* to growing this plant. Canada is also the world's largest exporter of mustard seed.

Name: _____

Are these nouns *singular* or *plural*?

1. oriole _____ lice _____

Underline the *prepositions* in each sentence. Circle the *object of each preposition*.

2. The new calf wobbled on its legs and fell down to the ground.

3. We found an old picture in a brass frame wrapped in an old newspaper.

Correct these sentences.

4. john franklin were an arctic exsplorer who tryed to find the northwest passage
   _____

5. in 1845 hims sips become trapt in the ise and his men was doomed to dye
   _____

WEEK 16
ACTIVITY 1
TOTAL /5

Name: _____

Circle the *subordinating conjunction* in this sentence.

1. Because she is such a good player, every team wants her.

Are the underlined verbs *transitive* or *intransitive*?

2. He <u>collapsed</u> at the end of the race. _____

3. The musician <u>picked</u> up his guitar and began to play.
   _____

Correct these sentences.

4. that there soop were cold but i eight it becuz i were sew hungry
   _____

5. benny who is my frend helped me rak the leafs and put them in them their baggs
   _____

WEEK 16
ACTIVITY 2
TOTAL /5

Name: _____

Circle the *antecedent* of the underlined pronouns.

1. This vase is fragile because it is very old.
2. Fannie has a job so she is making her own money now.

Circle the *correlative conjunctions* in this sentence.

3. Not only can Molly sing, but also she can dance.

Correct these sentences.

4. teddy red the retern adress on the envelope and open it imediately.
   _____

5. insid were a invitashun to a berthday party at cosmic werld extrem games
   _____

WEEK **16**
ACTIVITY **3**
TOTAL **/5**

Name: _____

Correct these sentences.

1. i has a knew mountin bik sew i wants to joyne the big bike cycling club
   _____

2. the rocky mountins they streches acrost british columbia and alberta
   _____

Underline the *simple subject* and circle the *simple predicate* in each sentence.

3. Glittering jewels and golden objects filled the treasure chest.
4. Mrs. Rogers teaches Celeste piano lessons.

How many syllables in each word?

5. responsibility _____   Athabasca _____

WEEK **16**
ACTIVITY **4**
TOTAL **/5**

Name: _____

Tell whether each sentence is *simple, compound* or *complex*.

WEEK 16

ACTIVITY 5

TOTAL /5

1. Sandy looked out the window but she didn't see her kitten. _____

2. Arlene has a new job in an office downtown. _____

3. They live in the city but they love the country. _____

4. When the phone rings, make sure you answer it. _____

5. If there is room on the bus, I will be going with you. _____

Name: _____

Bonus Activity: Up North Word Search

Find and circle the words shown in the box.

WEEK 16

i	n	u	k	s	h	u	k	i	h	y	w	i	a	d
n	i	k	o	a	s	g	r	e	b	e	c	i	y	o
u	e	c	a	s	e	y	t	o	r	b	s	h	t	g
i	f	a	s	m	i	d	e	e	g	c	m	m	a	s
t	f	r	p	m	k	c	t	r	d	x	l	f	s	l
n	e	i	l	m	s	c	e	b	o	m	a	t	i	e
b	m	b	r	i	u	e	t	f	r	e	m	a	s	d
h	n	o	r	t	h	e	r	n	l	i	g	h	t	s
t	f	u	p	k	a	s	m	i	u	o	v	p	j	a
l	r	r	a	e	b	r	a	l	o	p	e	m	l	g

huskies   caribou
dogsleds   icebergs
Sam McGee polar bear
Inuit   ice floe
inukshuk   fox
northern lights

MY CANADA *Monarch butterflies* make the longest migration of all insect species. They travel from Canada to Mexico, a distance of at least 4600 km, each fall.

Name: _____

WEEK 17
ACTIVITY 1

Correct these sentences.

1. the ferst inhabitints of canada comed frum asia thousends of year ago
   _____

2. erly exslporers called them indians we call them native people
   _____

TOTAL /5

Underline the *predicate adjectives* in each sentence.

3. They were very hot and thirsty after the game.

4. The sunset glowed red, orange and pink.

Is the verb in this sentence *transitive* or *intransitive*?

5. Several books are missing from my bookshelf. _____

Name: _____

WEEK 17
ACTIVITY 2

Underline the *objects of the prepositions* in these sentences.

1. Jenny received a card in the mail from her uncle in Dartmouth.

2. For the last time, put the cover on the pot and set it on the stove.

Correct these sentences.

3. the beutiful provence of british columbia are known for tall forists and tall mountins
   _____

TOTAL /5

4. becuz we was cookin mom opined the windows to gets sum frash air
   _____

Explain the meaning of this expression.

5. A stitch in time saves nine. _____

SSR1151 ISBN: 9781771587471 © On The Mark Press   55

Name: _____

WEEK 17 — ACTIVITY 3 — TOTAL /5

Circle the direct object and underline the indirect object.

1. We sent everyone in our family party invitations for Mom's birthday.

2. The babysitter made the children a good supper last night.

Add a prefix and a suffix to make a new word.

3. proper _____

Correct these sentences.

4. my littel cousen abby sings teddy bears picnic whil her is playing
   _____

5. her has a hole colleckshun of stuffed bares witch she has named
   _____

Name: _____

WEEK 17 — ACTIVITY 4 — TOTAL /5

Write the correct abbreviation for each word.

1. Lieutenant _____

2. Esquire _____

Correct these sentences.

3. were haveing a back sail to rase muney fore new instraments for hour sckool band
   _____

4. lee are the mostest talented musishun in fieldrow highs band
   _____

Complete the analogy.

5. Ping Pong is to paddle as _____ is to racquet.

Name: _____

Combine the following sentences to make one good sentence.

WEEK 17
ACTIVITY 5
TOTAL /5

1. We decided to go to dinner. We are going now. Are you coming with us?
   _____

2. Luke has a cold. He can't play in tonight's game. Don will have to play for him.
   _____

3. Cacti are hardy plants. They don't require much water. They are the best plants for me.
   _____

4. Ants crawled on the picnic table. They headed for the cake. Move the cake, quick!
   _____

5. My dog ran away. I couldn't stop him. He ran through the neighbour's flower bed.
   _____

Name: _____

Bonus Activity: Palindromes

WEEK 17

A *palindrome* is a word that is spelled the same forwards or backwards. **Complete the sentences below with palindromes.**

1. a short name for mother is _____

2. a short form for sister is _____

3. a needle has an _____

4. in the middle of the day, it is _____

5. Little birds make a sound called _____

6. That was really a funny _____

7. What _____ you do today?

8. The car will _____ its horn.

MY CANADA: The Montreal Metro is Canada's busiest subway system. An average of *1,241,000 people* travel to and from its 68 stations every day.

Name: _____

Are the following texts a *complete* sentence, or a *fragment*?

WEEK **18**

ACTIVITY **1**

1. Going to the Maritimes. _____

2. Herb is on his way here. _____

Correct these sentences.

TOTAL **/5**

3. michael wanted to bye knew pare of runing shoes they was two expensive

_____

4. that their old letter in my gramdmas trunk are dated may 21 1874

_____

Underline the helping, or *auxiliary*, verbs in this sentence.

5. We were thinking of you when you called.

Name: _____

Circle the *direct object* and underline the *indirect object*.

WEEK **18**

1. February will bring us more snow.

2. Did she tell you her secret?

ACTIVITY **2**

Correct these sentences.

TOTAL **/5**

3. you're projeckt on the avro arrow were exsellent ms herman told lila

_____

4. she worrys about evrything weather she have a reeson too ore not

_____

Circle the word with the most syllables.

5. anniversary   emergency   impersonate   observation

Name: _____

Correct these sentences.

1. serfers likes to stand on theyre bords and ride hi on the waves
   _____

2. the skared littel boy clinged to his mothers legs and woodn't go into the sckool
   _____

Circle the *subject pronoun* and underline the *object pronoun* in each sentence.

3. She told us all about her shopping trip to the mall.

4. I don't like hornets. One stung me yesterday on my arm.

Underline the *predicate adjectives* in this sentence.

5. Our town has an active, volunteer fire department.

WEEK 18
ACTIVITY 3
TOTAL /5

Name: _____

Circle the *subject* of this sentence.

1. Apply some sunscreen before going to the beach.   **we / he / it / you**

Correct these sentences.

2. on a hot humed day you shood stay in the shad and drinks lottsa water
   _____

3. marty thinked him heared a strange sound behind that there old shed
   _____

Complete these sentences with *who, which* or *that*.

4. Ella is someone _____ loves to cook for her family.

5. The Parliament Buildings, _____ are in Ottawa, are a great place to visit.

WEEK 18
ACTIVITY 4
TOTAL /5

Name: _____

Write the *simple subject* and the *simple predicate* in each sentence.

1. After practising every night, my brother made the team.

   Simple subject _____ **Simple predicate** _____

2. Because my dog has fleas, we bought special shampoo.

   Simple subject _____ **Simple predicate** _____

3. The big mother bear lumbered slowly along the path with her cubs.

   Simple subject _____ **Simple predicate** _____

4. Children who wash their hands often avoid catching colds.

   Simple subject _____ **Simple predicate** _____

5. The protesters marched along the street, carrying their picket signs.

   Simple subject _____ **Simple predicate** _____

WEEK 18
ACTIVITY 5
TOTAL /5

Name: _____

Bonus Activity: Context Clues

Write the meaning of the underlined word using the clues in the sentence.

1. He skis very well for a novice. _____

2. If it sounds too good to be true, it's probably a fraud. _____

3. If you are going to play the game, you must adhere to the rules.

   _____

4. The heat diminished as the sun went down. _____

5. The coach berated the players for being so careless.

   _____

WEEK 18

MY CANADA The oldest rocks on Earth are found in Canada. In fact, they are 250 million years older than other known rocks. In 2001, geologists found a 4.28 billion-year-old rock on the eastern shore of Hudson Bay, in northern Quebec.

Name: _____

WEEK 19
ACTIVITY 1
TOTAL /5

Correct these sentences.

1. yestarday we seen ron and serena at hour nayorhood pool with there parants
   _____

2. the andes moutins runned all the weigh down the cost of south america
   _____

Underline the *independent clause* in this sentence.

3. When our friends are in trouble, we try to help out.

Circle the best word to complete each sentence.

4. That soccer ball belongs to me. It is _____ **my / ours / us / mine**

5. This colourful kite belongs to Karen. It is _____ **them / their / hers / his**

Name: _____

WEEK 19
ACTIVITY 2
TOTAL /5

Rewrite this sentence to correct the run-on.

1. Mario played a good game he had a bad headache most of the time
   _____

Correct these sentences.

2. all that their constucktion make it very nosy in my nayborhood
   _____

3. kenneth waer in the wurld did you put them kees to my werkshoppe asked dad
   _____

Underline the *gerunds* in each sentence.

4. We like watching TV and playing games on the weekend.

5. Reading and writing are important skills to learn.

Name: _____

Underline the *correlative conjunctions* in this sentence.

1. Whether you go with us or stay home, you must decide soon.

Underline the *linking verb* in each sentence.

2. The sky grew darker and darker by the minute.

3. It became evident that we were getting a thunderstorm soon.

Correct these sentences.

4. the ferst coliny in canada were estableshed by the french on the bay of fundy

_____

5. the coliny were called acadia and the ferst setlment their were called port royal

_____

WEEK 19
ACTIVITY 3
TOTAL /5

Name: _____

Are these sentences *declarative, interrogative, imperative,* or *exclamatory*?

1. The sound of howling wolves could be heard at night.
   _____

2. Are you afraid they will come to close to the cabin? _____

Underline the *subordinate clause* in this sentence.

3. Unless we start to work faster, we won't finish this job on time.

Correct these sentences.

4. sharon loked in desgust at the miss in the living room her bothers had maid

_____

5. patata chip crums, pizza crusts emty pop cans and plats was evrywear

_____

WEEK 19
ACTIVITY 4
TOTAL /5

Name: _____

WEEK 19

Some adjectives have *irregular comparisons*. **Write the correct form of the adjective on the line.**

ACTIVITY 5

1. My money is almost all gone. I have even _____ than last week. *(little)*

2. Ted has _____ trading cards but Larry has the _____ . *(many)*

TOTAL /5

3. My grandma is feeling _____ now that she has seen her doctor. *(good)*

4. The weather is really turning _____. This may be the _____ storm ever. *(bad)*

5. I have _____ math mistakes but Henry has the _____ . *(some)*

Name: _____

WEEK 19

Bonus Activity: Idioms

Explain the meaning of the underlined idioms.

1. You are winning so far but don't push your luck. _____

2. Is that story true or are you putting me on? _____

3. That chocolate cream pie is out of this world. _____

4. Stick together. We're all in the same boat. _____

5. Jed was called up on the carpet for his actions. _____

MY CANADA — The largest colony of red-sided garter snakes in the world lives 90 miles north of Winnipeg. In late April or early May, tens of thousands of these snakes come out off their homes in the Narcisse Snake Dens and congregate at the surface.

Name: _____

Circle the *antecedent* of the underlined pronoun.

1. Rob and Lori love <u>their</u> new pet puppy. _____

Underline the *adverbs* in each sentence. Do they tell *how, where, when* or to *what extent*?

2. I received your message late and could not answer. _____

3. Mr. Bronson was quite happy with my performance in the play. _____

Correct these sentences.

4. the boy want a cap simlar too the won him have lost
   _____

5. it have the name of hims favrite basball teem the toronto blue jays
   _____

WEEK 20
ACTIVITY 1
TOTAL /5

Name: _____

Correct these sentences.

1. the originel johhny canuck appered in newspaper cartunes in the 1880s
   _____

2. the talltail hero dressed as a lumbrjack a fermer and somtimes as a ranchir
   _____

Underline the *adjective clause* in each sentence.

3. The windows that face the east will let in the most sunshine.

4. The lake where we caught all the fish is our secret.

Underline the subject of this sentence.

5. Pat, who is my neighbour, walks her dog four times a day.

WEEK 20
ACTIVITY 2
TOTAL /5

Name: _____

Underline the *subordinating conjunction* in this sentence.

1. Although I believe your story, others may not.

Correct these sentences.

2. my cuzin kenton b thomas are a reporter for the vancouver sun
   _____

3. wunce him let me go with him to intervue a famus misstery righter
   _____

Underline the *indefinite pronoun* in each sentence.

4. Many of the children would like to go to summer camp.

5. The supervisor will speak to anyone who is interested.

WEEK **20**

ACTIVITY **3**

TOTAL **/5**

Name: _____

Circle the *subject pronoun* and underline the *object pronoun* in each sentence.

1. We will pick them up after school today.

2. They hit us with snowballs when we weren't looking.

Correct these sentences.

3. we is reedin a good book in hour english class with mr hudson
   _____

4. it is called undergound to canada is the story of harriet tubman
   _____

Underline the *personified word* in this sentence.

5. The wind grabbed the papers from my hand.

WEEK **20**

ACTIVITY **4**

TOTAL **/5**

Name: _____

Rewrite the following sentences to punctuate the dialogue correctly.

WEEK 20
ACTIVITY 5
TOTAL /5

1. Mom I'm home from school Theo called can I have a snack

   _____

2. Let's watch this program Reagan suggested it's called the history of rock and roll

   _____

3. The principal began today we have a serious matter to discuss with all of you

   _____

4. Will you be here when Gwen's parents arrive inquired her aunt sadie

   _____

5. I want to tell you about my hobby artie said i collect old comic books

   _____

Name: _____

Bonus Activity: A is for …

Number these words in alphabetical order.

____ absurd	____ argument	____ ahoy
____ abide	____ applicant	____ abandon
____ agility	____ abacus	____ amiable
____ athlete	____ abnormal	____ alert
____ aerial	____ about-face	____ appreciate
____ ancient	____ awesome	____ affirm
____ antagonist	____ axe	____ azure
____ accident	____ airsick	____ auditory

MY CANADA   *Pingos* are unusual, earth-covered mounds of ice. One-fourth of the world's pingos, 1350 of them, can be found on the Tuktoyaktok Peninsula in the western Arctic. Each one lasts about 1000 years before breaking down.

Name: _____

Circle the *antecedent* of the underlined pronoun.

1. Marion is good company because <u>she</u> is so funny.

2. My dad, who has started a new job, has <u>his</u> office in downtown Winnipeg.

Correct these sentences.

3. becuz of the blizerd we mist playing our rivel team the falcons
   _____

4. does you think we had a chanse of beeting them asked perry
   _____

Circle the *coordinating conjunctions* in this sentence.

5. We are all ready so let's go outside.

WEEK 21
ACTIVITY 1
TOTAL /5

Name: _____

Correct these sentences.

1. williams family moved to swift current saskatchewan on june 29 2013
   _____

2. does you smell that delishus odor asked jon sumone is barbequeing bergers
   _____

Underline the *abstract nouns* in these sentences.

3. Good manners will always be valued and respected.

4. Peter's charm and good humour have made him popular.

Is this sentence *simple, compound* or *complex*?

5. Allie likes to visit the city so she can go to see a live performance.
   _____

WEEK 21
ACTIVITY 2
TOTAL /5

Name: _____

Write the *superlative* and *comparative* forms of this adjective.

1. stormy _____ _____

Correct these sentences.

2. i has jist finished reading a book called secrets of the frozen seas said mark
   _____

3. it telled of brave exsplorers trying to travel acrost the icey lands of canada's arctic
   _____

Is the following text a *complete* sentence, or a *fragment*?

4. I don't got no time.   _____

5. He don't have nowhere to go.   _____

WEEK 21
ACTIVITY 3
TOTAL /5

Name: _____

Correct these sentences.

1. ed needs to gets a job and safe lottsa money to go on the studant exschange
   _____

2. hims class wants to pare up with a school in moosonee ontario
   _____

Is the predicate in each sentence *simple* or *compound*?

3. Birds work very hard to build safe nests for their eggs. _____

4. They choose a good location, collect materials and set to work. _____

Choose the best word to complete this sentence.

5. You will have to work _____ next term.   **more hard / more harder / harder**

WEEK 21
ACTIVITY 4
TOTAL /5

Name: _____

Combine the following sentences to make one good sentence.

WEEK 21
ACTIVITY 5
TOTAL /5

1. We had a bad storm last night. It was thundering and lightning. Our pets were afraid.

   _____

2. I can't meet you at noon today. I have a job interview. I will see you later.

   _____

3. The horses reached the cool stream. They were hot and thirsty. They stopped to drink.

   _____

4. Lois hasn't phoned us for two weeks. She hasn't texted us either. We are worried about her.

   _____

Name: _____

Bonus Activity: Animal Idioms

WEEK 21

These idioms use the names of animals in their expression. **Write your own explanation of the underlined idioms.**

1. I had butterflies in my stomach when I was saying my speech in class.

   _____

2. What a crazy idea! Does he have bats in his belfry?

   _____

3. Be careful what you tell Savannah. She tends to be catty.

   _____

Early explorer, Henry Hudson was obsessed with finding the Northwest Passage. In 1611, after spending a harsh winter locked in iced, his crew wanted to return home. When Hudson refused, they put him and his son into a small open boat and set them adrift. They were never heard of again.

MY CANADA

Name: _____

Underline the *infinitives* in each sentence.

1. I did not dare to speak while dad was scolding me.

2. Several people stepped forward to help the stranger.

How many syllables does this word have?

3. Miramichi   _____

Correct these sentences.

4. the short quite boy standed by the fense watching the boys play socer

   _____

5. joelle are working more hard then ever to make the cheerleeding teem

   _____

WEEK 22
ACTIVITY 1
TOTAL /5

Name: _____

Underline the *verbs* in this sentence. Then name the tense.

1. After the play ended, the audience clapped. _____

Underline the *subordinate clause* in each sentence.

2. When the oven is hot enough, put in the casserole.

3. Jaxon left before I had a chance to ask him about our homework.

Correct these sentences.

4. gram said life were more harder yeers ago but we had lottsa famly fun

   _____

5. we evan managed to gets along with out a telaphone or telavisen she chuckled

   _____

WEEK 22
ACTIVITY 2
TOTAL /5

Name: _____

WEEK 22
ACTIVITY 3
TOTAL /5

Underline the *subordinating conjunction* in each sentence.

1. While we were on vacation, we made many new friends.

2. I will help him with his math because he asked me.

Circle the words that have four syllables.

3. disastrous   haberdasher   lamination   management

Correct these sentences.

4. the belcher islands located in hudson bay belongs to nunavut

   _____

5. nest weak hour class are reeding shakepeare's play romeo and juliet

   _____

Name: _____

WEEK 22
ACTIVITY 4
TOTAL /5

Underline the *linking verb* in this sentence.

1. My kitten seems ill because it won't even drink water.

   _____

Correct these sentences.

2. jane who am my bestest frend were elected president of the stewdent counsel

   _____

3. everybody who know her were suprised when her quite the baskitball team

   _____

Underline the predicate adjectives in each sentence.

4. Those brownies are sweet, chocolatey, and delicious.

   _____

5. The children seem happy and contented in their new home.

   _____

Name: _____

Rewrite this short paragraph, correcting all the punctuation errors.

john cabot an italian explorer may have landed on the shores of newfoundland or nova scotia he claimed the land for king henry of england and began his journey home his ship the matthew crossed over the grand banks and came upon great schools of cod fish the crew wanted to catch some to provide a food supply for the long voyage at first their methods proved unsuccessful then one sailor suggested let us try baskets the idea worked and the crew were rewarded with tons of gleaming fish

WEEK 22

ACTIVITY 5

TOTAL /5

_____
_____
_____
_____
_____
_____
_____

Name: _____

Bonus Activity: What's Next?

Finish the story below by writing a short conclusion. Illustrate the story.

Dave and Aiden were bored at the farm so they decided to explore the nearby woods. At first it was great. They ran along the path, checked out a rotted log and followed some rabbit tracks for a while. By the time they realized that it was getting dark, they discovered they had left the path. Everything looked the same and it was beginning to snow. "This doesn't look good," said Dave.

WEEK 22

BONUS ACTIVITY

My Conclusion   **My Illustration**

_____
_____
_____
_____

Dr. Joseph MacInnis built the world's first polar undersea station in 1972. Located under the Northwest Passage, the capsule, nicknamed Sub-Igloo, had enough room for four people.

MY CANADA

Name: _____

Correct these sentences.

WEEK **23**

1. wen all that their snow falled the path to the street becomed invisable

   _____

2. the bay were chopy and dangrous as them fishin boats perpared to set out

   _____

ACTIVITY **1**

TOTAL **/5**

Underline the *adjective phrase* in this sentence.

3. A cowboy on a horse appeared on the horizon.

Circle the *antecedent* of the underlined pronoun.

4. The mother dog bunched up a blanket to cover her newborn puppies.

5. Jade sent a gift to her cousin in Edmonton.

Name: _____

Correct these sentences.

WEEK **23**

1. did you notice them fans setting near us waring ottawa senators gerseys

   _____

2. wen i get my pay check i'll put sum muney in the bank and spend sum on treets

   _____

ACTIVITY **2**

TOTAL **/5**

Underline the *simple subject* in each sentence.

3. Many people live in large cities.

4. Our kitchen is our family meeting place.

Circle the *prefix* that means "not"

5.   co   pre   im   non

Name: _____

Correct these sentences.

1. the crowed screemed go kyle go as him rushed toword the net with the ball
   _____

2. the led sanger of the all girl band street angels singed my favorit song
   _____

Underline the *abstract nouns* in this sentence.

3. It takes a lot of energy and determination to succeed in sports.

Underline the *predicate adjectives* in each sentence.

4. His dog, Duke, is faithful and loyal.

5. The clouds looked dark and ominous.

WEEK 23
ACTIVITY 3
TOTAL /5

Name: _____

Add the same *suffix* to each base to make a new word

1. kilo_____   tele_____

Is the underlined verb transitive or intransitive?

2. Locks and keys <u>keep</u> our possessions safe.

3. Vines <u>climb</u> along fences or poles.

Correct these sentences.

4. british columbia are the western most provence in canada
   _____

5. british columbia have a warmer climet witch make it a poplar place to live
   _____

WEEK 23
ACTIVITY 4
TOTAL /5

Name: _____

Read each sentence. Write the sentence parts listed.

1. My uncle constructed a greenhouse with glass windows and a glass roof.

Simple subject _____   *Simple predicate* _____

2. Its simple construction is its best feature.

Pronoun _____   *Antecedent* _____

3. He gives the plants the best care so they can thrive.

Direct object _____   *Indirect object* _____

4. Our whole family helps to spray any bugs that appear.

Complete subject _____   *Simple predicate* _____

5. You can harvest vegetables in a greenhouse.

Preposition _____   *Object of a preposition* _____

WEEK 23
ACTIVITY 5
TOTAL /5

Name: _____

Bonus Activity: Homophones Crossword

Homophones sound the same but have different spellings and meanings. **Choose the correct homophone to match the clue.**

Across
1. cook the (meat, meet)
2. you should not (steel, steal)
3. tell a tall (tail, tale)
4. don't (meddle, medal) in my business
5. she is too (week, weak) to walk
6. did you (here, hear) the phone?
7. put some (wood, would) on the fire

Down
1. the old car had to be (toad, towed)
2. it is rude to (stare, stair)
4. brush the horse's (mane, main)
5. use (flower, flour) for baking
6. (pore, pour) water into the bottle

WEEK 23
BONUS ACTIVITY

MY CANADA

The *first Canadian race car driver* to win the Grand Prix was Gilles Villeneuve in Montreal on Oct. 8, 1978. He was born in Chambly, Quebec on January 18, 1950 and sadly, died in a crash while trying to qualify for the Belgium Grand Prix on May 8, 1982.

Name: _____

WEEK 24
ACTIVITY 1
TOTAL /5

Circle the best word to complete this sentence.

1. I have my friends and my sister has _____ .   **her / she / hers / them**

Correct these sentences.

2. my dads army foto show him standing between his fellow solders at cfb kingston
   _____

3. altho i likes that knew band i probly woodn't bye there currant cd look at this
   _____

Underline the word that is personified in each sentence.

4. Time marches on and waits for no one.

5. Our hedge was standing knee deep in snow.

Name: _____

WEEK 24
ACTIVITY 2
TOTAL /5

Underline the *subject*. Tell whether it is *simple* or *compound*.

1. The buffet table was loaded with good things to eat.   _____

2. Roast chicken, salad, and fresh buns caught my eye.   _____

Correct these sentences.

3. i has a frend john and he lives down the street and he are in my classe
   _____

4. last nite the skye were cloud less the big dipper standed out quit planely
   _____

Underline the *adverbs* in this sentence.

5. Quickly, yet stealthily, Joanne hid the present that she bought yesterday.

Name: _____

Write the plural form of this noun.

1. oasis _____

Correct these sentences.

2. this here years basketball champiunship turnament are being held at redford high
_____

3. me and gary watched a intresting show on nat geo wild called under the ice cap
_____

Insert the commas in their correct places in each sentence.

4. Harry close the door please.

5. The spring months are March April and May.

WEEK 24
ACTIVITY 3
TOTAL /5

Name: _____

Correct these sentences.

1. as the storm approched the animils taked sheltar under the big oke trees
_____

2. a blankit of frash snow lie deep on the roove of vacent old house
_____

Underline the *prepositional phrases* in each sentence.

3. He ran across the road, through the barnyard, and into the stable.

4. We sat in front of the open fire, watching the dance of the flames.

Is this sentence *declarative*, *interrogative*, *imperative*, or *exclamatory*?

5. Call me as soon as you hear about your job interview.

WEEK 24
ACTIVITY 4
TOTAL /5

Name: _____

A *verb* is in *active voice* when the subject is performing the action. A *verb* is in *passive voice* when the subject is receiving the action. **Tell whether each verb is in active or passive voice. Then rewrite the sentence to change the verb voice.**

1. Heavy clouds hid the sun. _____
   _____

2. The house was struck by lightning. _____
   _____

3. The teacher gave Caleb the prize. _____
   _____

4. Aunt Cassie sent me a birthday present. _____
   _____

5. He was seen leaving the theatre by two people. _____
   _____

Name: _____

Bonus Activity: It's All About Food

Place the following words in each of the categories below.

freeze, kitchen, stove, cupboard, drive-through, pot, microwave oven, bag, nibble, canteen, freezer, chew, frying pan, cafeteria, roast, barbeque, box, broil, refrigerator, picnic table, toaster, restaurant, jar, prepare

Where We Keep Food	Places to Eat Food	What We Do to Food	Items to Help Us Cook

MY CANDADA

The first Canadian athlete to appear on the front of an American cereal box was figure skater Kurt Browning. He was shown on the front of Special K boxes in 1998.

Name: _____

Correct these sentences.

WEEK **25**

ACTIVITY **1**

1. in hisstory class today we lernt about amelia earhart a couragus pilot
   _____

2. as the ferst woman to fly over the atlantic osean she were admired by meny people
   _____

TOTAL /5

Underline the *subordinate clause* in each sentence.

3. Sarah covered her eyes while we were watching the monster movie.

4. After it was over, she declared she was never afraid.

Underline the *phrases* in this sentence.

5. Pete and Hallie went to the amusement park and rode on the roller coaster.

Name: _____

Correct these sentences.

WEEK **25**

ACTIVITY **2**

1. arent the davidsons new house in that there sub division on monarch drive
   _____

2. yes i thinks you is corect replyed harrison they moved their last saturday
   _____

TOTAL /5

Underline the *collective nouns* in this sentence.

3. The audience clapped when the choir finished the final performance.

How many syllables in each word?

4. Mt. Nesselrode _____

5. Matagami _____

Name: _____

Underline the *present participle* in each sentence.

1. Willy is telling a different story than you are telling.

2. We are leaving right now so get ready please.

Correct these sentences.

3. the top mostest speed on that there hiway are 100 kilos par hour
   _____

4. if you exseed that limet you will be find and mabe loose points on yore license
   _____

Rewrite this phrase using a *possessive noun*.

5. the surprise party for my parents _____

WEEK 25
ACTIVITY 3
TOTAL /5

Name: _____

Correct these sentences.

1. even tho moms car are newer then dads her have the highest number of kilometers
   _____

2. flower egg vineger and shortning is used in this here pye crust recipey
   _____

Write the *root* word for:

3. perfectionist _____

Underline the *independent clause* in each sentence.

4. I need to sharpen my skates before I can go skating with you.

5. As soon as he realized they were missing, Jared starting looking for his keys.

WEEK 25
ACTIVITY 4
TOTAL /5

Name: _____

An *appositive phrase* gives information about the word immediately before it.
Underline the appositive phrase in each sentence, and insert needed commas.

WEEK **25**

ACTIVITY **5**

TOTAL **/5**

1. Johnny Brown a rookie on our hockey team is a great asset to the game.

2. My favourite exercise playing on a soccer team helps keep me in shape.

3. Jace's ultimate goal to go to medical school is the reason he works so hard.

4. My uncle a longtime world traveller has many exciting tales to tell our family.

5. Their journey starting out as a short one soon became more and more lengthy.

Name: _____

Bonus Activity: Steve Nash

Read the paragraph. Circle T if the sentence is true and F if it is false.

WEEK **25**

Steve Nash is a well-known and well-liked Canadian athlete. He was the first Canadian to win the Most Valuable Player Award in the National Basketball Association. The Vancouver native received the award in the 2004-2005 season and then won it again in the following year! Adding to this, only eight other players have won back-to-back MVP awards in the league's history and only two other guards have won multiple times. Today, Steve Nash is still active in the sport, coaching and mentoring young players.

1. T F Steve Nash won MVP three years in a row.
2. T F He plays the position of guard on his team.
3. T F Steve Nash was born in Toronto, Ontario.

MY CANADA

The *Elmira Maple Syrup Festival* was recognized by the Guinness World Records in 2000 as the world's largest single-day maple syrup festival. There were 66,529 people attending the event that year. Sweet!

Name: _____

WEEK 26

ACTIVITY 1

TOTAL /5

Explain these idioms.

1. This is my fault so I will face the music. _____

2. Lying just takes you out of the frying pan into the fire. _____

Correct these sentences.

3. where'd you learn to play the piano so good asked freddy
   _____

4. commershell jets is seldum struck by lighting but terbulance are a problum
   _____

Circle the *antecedent* of the underlined pronoun.

5. That new grocery store is very clean and its produce selection is excellent.

Name: _____

WEEK 26

ACTIVITY 2

TOTAL /5

Complete each sentence with *who, which* or *that*.

1. Anita, _____ is my best friend, is moving away in August.

2. Provincial parks, _____ are owned by the government, are great to visit.

Is the underlined text a *simile* or a *metaphor*?

3. The field was a sea of sunflowers. _____

Correct these sentences.

4. nanook of the north a silint movie were about a group of inuit liveing along hudson bay
   _____

5. maid in 1922 it were recognised as the ferst full length dockumentairy film
   _____

Name: _____

WEEK 26 — ACTIVITY 3 — TOTAL /5

Underline the *independent clause* in each sentence.

1. After three attempts to climb the mountain, Kelly gave up.

2. I love soup for lunch, especially if it is homemade.

Correct these sentences.

3. i allways has to reed the three little pigs to my cousen when i babyset hims
   _____

4. june 22 2016 will be graderation day for my classmats and me
   _____

Is the tense of the verb in this sentence *past*, *present*, or *future*?

5. Will you be able to help me with my project? _____

Name: _____

WEEK 26 — ACTIVITY 4 — TOTAL /5

Correct these sentences.

1. casey at the bat ritten by ernest l thayer are a funny pome about a baseball player
   _____

2. it shos us what can happin when a persen is two arrogent and have foolish pride
   _____

Write the correct form of the *adjective* in each sentences.

3. This is the _____ storm we have had this winter. *(bad)*

4. I love chocolate cake! It's the _____ ! *(good)*

Underline the *simple subject* and circle the *simple predicate* in this sentence.

5. My dreams for the future involves travel and making new friends.

Name: _____

Rewrite these sentences putting in parentheses where needed.

1. Please note that this cheque is for one hundred 100 dollars.
   _____

2. There is new research available on the West Nile virus from the WHO World Health Organization.
   _____

3. My cousin Barb who is also my best friend is teaching me to play the clarinet.
   _____

4. Originally there were only six teams in the NHL National Hockey League.
   _____

5. Sir. John A. Macdonald 1815 – 1891 was a colourful character in our history.
   _____

WEEK **26**

ACTIVITY **5**

TOTAL **/5**

Name: _____

Bonus Activity: Extra! Extra!

Imagine that fairy tale stories are actually true and you are a reporter given the task of writing headlines for them. **Write a catchy and humorous headline for each of these stories.** Remember to use the proper punctuation.
Example: Sleeping Beauty: Castle Life Halted by Sleeping Princess

1. Jack and the Beanstalk: _____

2. Snow White: _____

3. Beauty and the Beast: _____

4. The Three Little Pigs: _____

WEEK **26**

BONUS ACTIVITY

MY CANADA

Niagara Falls – beautiful but dangerous! Daredevils are often tempted to try to go over the Falls as a thrill. In 1901, Annie Taylor was the first person to go over the Falls in a barrel and survive. Many others followed, most of them losing their lives and or never being found.

Name: _____

WEEK 27
ACTIVITY 1
TOTAL /5

Correct these sentences.

1. strawbarries is my favrit kind of fruit i eats alot of thum when their in seeson

   _____

2. my frend marla lives on the forth floor of the billding rite next to the j h newton libary

   _____

Underline the *predicate adjectives* in each sentence.

3. Pug puppies are so friendly, adorable and loving.

4. The mother bear was fearless and relentless in her fight to protect her cub.

Is this sentence *declarative, interrogative, imperative,* or *exclamatory*?

5. "Has anyone seen my reading glasses?" asked Grandpa Bill. _____

Name: _____

WEEK 27
ACTIVITY 2
TOTAL /5

Underline the *direct object* and circle the *indirect object* in each sentence.

1. Chris told his friends all about his vacation plans.

2. I tossed my little cousin the ball as gently as I could.

Number these words in alphabetical order

3. ___ confront ___ concave ___ condemn ___ convey ___ contrast ___ convince

Correct these sentences.

4. famus country western singers appeer at the calgary stampede each year

   _____

5. because she moved to new brunswick in grade 3 cheryl speak french real good

   _____

Name: _____

Use context clues to explain the meaning of the underlined words.

1. My little brother is tired, sick and <u>peevish</u>.

   _____

2. Most people consider swearing to be quite <u>vulgar</u>.

   _____

Correct these sentences.

3. look this here way and smile dont blink the fotographer said to our class

   _____

4. all them tv netwerks is carrying the story of the brave rescue by the ski petrol

   _____

Circle the *prefix* that means "under"

5. con   post   sub   un

WEEK 27
ACTIVITY 3
TOTAL /5

Name: _____

Explain the meaning of this idiom.

1. Sherry was <u>down in the dumps</u> when she heard the news.

Correct these sentences.

2. the junior players troop is performing a play called to be a child on sunday

   _____

3. the final seen will bee performed by the entir cast they is all on stage at wunce

   _____

Tell if the sentence is *simple, compound,* or *complex*.

4. Mom went shopping because we needed groceries. _____

5. Finish your homework, take a shower and go to bed. _____

WEEK 27
ACTIVITY 4
TOTAL /5

Name: _____

Correct the errors in this business letter. Write each underlined part correctly.

(1) january 27 2016

(2) dear ms radford

(3) thank you for coming to our school today to help us celebrate **(4)** family literacy day. The students enjoyed the copies of the puzzles you brought to share. Please feel welcome to visit our school again sometime.

(5) your truly

Elaine Barham

1. _____   4. _____

2. _____   5. _____

3. _____

WEEK 27

ACTIVITY 5

TOTAL /5

Name: _____

Bonus Activity: Islands

Canada is home to many big islands. **Find the following words in the puzzle.**

AKIMISKI	ELLESMERE
NTICOSTI	MAGDALEN
BAFFIN	MANITOULIN
BANKS	VANCOUVER
BELCHER	VICTORIA

V	A	N	C	O	U	V	E	C	R	B	E
B	I	T	B	A	N	K	S	T	B	C	R
E	N	C	A	B	C	T	S	F	W	H	E
L	E	O	T	L	I	O	V	E	O	B	M
C	L	N	T	O	C	H	E	H	I	A	S
H	A	L	L	I	R	S	W	M	B	F	E
E	D	A	T	A	W	I	O	R	T	F	L
R	G	N	W	O	B	E	A	N	N	I	L
M	A	N	I	T	O	U	L	I	N	N	E
O	M	A	I	K	S	I	M	I	K	A	H

WEEK 27

The largest freshwater sandbar and dune in the world can be found near Belleville, Ontario. Erosion caused the dunes to grow remarkably fast. In the early 1960s, the Sandbanks Provincial Park opened to the public.

MY CANADA

Name: _____

Underline the *gerunds* in each sentence.

1. Swimming and diving are Theo's best sports.

2. Waiting for us to get ready was making Mom impatient.

Correct these sentences.

3. them socer cleets look real good but their two expensive for me to bye
   _____

4. why doesnt you use sum of yore berthday muney asked victer
   _____

How many syllables in these place names?

5. Buffalo Narrows _____   Ungava Peninsula _____

WEEK 28
ACTIVITY 1
TOTAL /5

Name: _____

Write a contraction for the underlined words.

1. Lily said <u>she would</u> help me finish the posters for the bake sale. _____

Correct these sentences.

2. quinn does you want to go to the boys and girls club tonite asked wanda
   _____

3. they is gonna learn us a new danse and show us how to cook lessagna
   _____

Underline the *predicate adjectives*.

4. That poor stray dog looks mangy, underfed and unwell.

5. Spring weather is warm, fresh and inviting.

WEEK 28
ACTIVITY 2
TOTAL /5

Name: _____

Underline the *prepositional phrase* and circle the *direct object* of the preposition.

1. A cruise from Vancouver to Alaska is one of the most beautiful trips.

2. Laws are made by the people and for the good of the people.

Underline the *antonyms* in the following sentence.

3. Remember Elton is innocent until proven guilty.

Correct these sentences.

4. randall is a intelligant boy but sumtimes him cans be vary rood to others

   _____

5. suger froot and nuts give flaver to ice creem egg and gelitin makes it smooth

   _____

WEEK **28**

ACTIVITY **3**

TOTAL **/5**

Name: _____

Write the plural for these nouns.

1. half _____   sheep _____

Correct these sentences.

2. what a day of wilde whether we had snow wind and freesing rein remarked yanni

   _____

3. meny people loves winter sports sking snowshooing skateing and ise fishin

   _____

Tell the gender of these nouns. Write M for Masculine, F for Female, or N for Neuter

4. emperor _____

5. statue _____

WEEK **28**

ACTIVITY **4**

TOTAL **/5**

Name: _____

Combine the following sentences to make one good sentence.

1. British Columbia is a Canadian province. It is the western-most province. One of its borders is the Pacific Ocean.

   _____

2. Captain Cook landed on Vancouver island. He landed about 200 years ago. He traded goods for furs with the native people.

   _____

3. People work in many industries. Some people work in sawmills, wood factories and fish canneries. Some people work in the vast forests.

   _____

4. British Columbia is extremely mountainous. The Rocky Mountains run through the province. The mountains create beautiful scenery.

   _____

WEEK 28
ACTIVITY 5
TOTAL /5

Name: _____

Bonus Activity: Drink Up!

Read the table that lists the ingredients in four popular drinks. Then circle T for TRUE and F for FALSE for each statement.

Beverage	Ingredient #1: Sugar	Ingredient #2: Sodium	Ingredient #3: Carbohydrates	Calories per 250 ml
A	23 g	38 mg	23 g	100
B	25g	30 mg	25 g	100
C	30g	10 mg	30 g	108
D	26g	170 mg	26 g	160

1. T F   All four drinks have the same amount of sugar.
2. T F   It takes about 375 ml of Drinks A, B, and C to equal the calories in Drink D.
3. T F   The healthiest drink choice is Drink C.

MY CANADA   *Newfoundland and Labrador* have their own time zone called Newfoundland Standard Time which it shares with no other inhabited region. It calculates its time to be 30 minutes ahead of Atlantic Standard Time.

WEEK 29 — ACTIVITY 1

Correct these sentences.

1. mr keyes exsplantion of the combushun ingine wear clear and consise

2. ingrid and olive who is patty's best frends said she wood be glad to help out

Fill in the correct past participle for the given verb.

3. Lighthouses have _____ out signals to ships to guide them. *(send)*

4. Lighthouses have _____ ships out of danger. *(keep)*

Underline the *subordinate clause* in this sentence.

5. I never talk to Mom until she has had her first cup of coffee.

TOTAL /5

WEEK 29 — ACTIVITY 2

Correct these sentences.

1. the jery couldnt reech a unanimus desision so it were a hanged jery

2. anaka studyed piano with ms dreyfus fore six yeers her hard werk have payed off

Use context clues to explain the meaning of the underlined words.

3. They buy many <u>souvenirs</u> while on vacation.

4. Climbing up the wet and winding path was <u>treacherous</u>.

***Synonyms* or *antonyms*?**

5. intricate, complicated _____

TOTAL /5

Name: _____

Correct these sentences.

WEEK 29
ACTIVITY 3
TOTAL /5

1. robyns blew jays chickades and sparrows all visits grandpas berd feaders

   _____

2. whose the generus person that sended me these her movie tickets me whisperd

   _____

Underline the *linking verb* in each sentence.

3. The thunder appeared to be a warning of the coming storm.

4. The windshield looked like frosted glass.

Is the underlined text a *complete* sentence, or *fragment*?

5. Sandra works in a medical lab. Searching for a cure. _____

Name: _____

Underline the *preposition* and circle the *object of the preposition* in each sentence.

WEEK 29
ACTIVITY 4
TOTAL /5

1. My grandparents are amazed by the progress in everyday technology.

2. They built their house on high ground in a sheltered area.

Correct these sentences.

3. the bayview community hall were builded in august 2009 neer hour school

   _____

4. ofen ant dolly like to set on her front poarch and reed her sowing magizines

   _____

Underline the *interjection* in this sentence.

5. Oh great! Now I have to babysit my baby brother!

Name: _____

Rewrite these sentences to correctly punctuate the dialogue.

WEEK 29

ACTIVITY 5

TOTAL /5

1. Come again said Petra when you can stay longer and visit
   _____

2. Hey Larry shouted wait for me I'll be right there.
   _____

3. I didn't mean to lose your bracelet I said to my sister will you forgive me
   _____

4. Try this flavour of ice cream suggested Connie it's called spumoni
   _____

5. I hope you are hungry said dad because I am in the mood to barbeque
   _____

Name: _____

Bonus Activity: Where Do I Look?

WEEK 29

BONUS ACTIVITY

There are many sources of information we can use. **Pick a reference source from this list to match the phrases to tell where you would look for information.**

| encyclopedia | cookbook | atlas | thesaurus | dictionary | almanac |

1. the location of Fort Resolution _____

2. a description of the inside of a long house _____

3. another word for "hypocrite" _____

4. the pronunciation of "gourmet" _____

5. an antonym for " luminous" _____

MY CANDA *Bulk Barn* is Canada's largest bulk food retailer. Opening in 1982, the stores offer everything from soup to nuts and spices and candy and baking supplies and cereals and …

WEEK 30 — ACTIVITY 1

Add a suffix to each verb to make it into a noun.

1. excite _____   appear _____

Correct these sentences.

2. hour neighbor mr benson have the bigger and bestest gardin on hour street
   _____

3. its hims hobby sew he give much of hims harvist to his luky neighbors
   _____

Circle the *antecedent* of the underlined pronoun.

4. When the towels were dry, we removed <u>them</u> from the clothes dryer.

5. The Lunch Box serves <u>its</u> meals faster than other places.

TOTAL /5

WEEK 30 — ACTIVITY 2

Is the underlined verb *transitive* or *intransitive*?

1. Elliott <u>reads</u> the online newspaper everyday. _____

Correct these sentences.

2. eddie is my nicname the girl explained but my reel name is edwina
   _____

3. his frends allways teese nick about his read hare but he just laugh
   _____

Circle the best word to complete each sentence.

4. These keys belong to Aunt Freda. They are ____.   **her / theirs / hers / their**

5. That wallet belongs to Mr. Bennett. It is ____.   **him / ours / his / our**

TOTAL /5

Name: _____

Correct these sentences.

1. we all has knew scarfs and hats mine are red and my bothers is blew
   _____

2. zoe are goin hikeing next wekend kara are goin two they go together
   _____

Underline the *abstract nouns* in this sentence.

3. There is no substitute for intelligence, enthusiasm, and honesty.

Tell if each sentence is *declarative, exclamatory, imperative,* or *interrogative*.

4. When the water boils, make the tea.   _____

5. Nobody saw the person who stole the money.   _____

WEEK **30**
ACTIVITY **3**
TOTAL **/5**

Name: _____

Correct these sentences.

1. its not fare said jerome that i has to miss the bestest movie of the yeer
   _____

2. if your hungary has a lite snak sew you didn't spoil you're diner
   _____

Write the base, or *root*, word for this word.

3. unlikelihood _____

Circle the best word to complete each sentence.

4. Lanny is the _____ walker I know.   **slower / slowly / slowest / most slowly**

5. You eat _____ than most people.   **quickly / quickest / most quickly / quicker**

WEEK **30**
ACTIVITY **4**
TOTAL **/5**

Name: _____

Some pairs of words are easily confused. Read the word pair at the end of each sentence. Then write the correct word on the blank.

WEEK **30**

ACTIVITY **5**

TOTAL **/5**

1. If you like chicken soup better _____ tomato, _____ have the kind you prefer. *(then, than)*

2. _____ a shame you dog doesn't like _____ new collar. *(its, it's)*

3. Leave _____ mail over _____ on the table. *(their, there)*

4. _____ jacket is this and _____ going to return it? *(who's, whose)*

5. We are _____ to leave and you have spilled something on your shirt. _____ *(all ready, already)*

Name: _____

WEEK **30**

Bonus Activity: Animals Everywhere

Place the following words in each of the categories below.

boar, hare, newt, weasel, wolverine, badger, ewe, caribou, polliwog, stallion, buffalo, heifer, reindeer, whale, pika, walrus, grizzly bear, kid, gopher, lobster, muskox, marmot, seal, foal

Farm Animals	Small Wild Animals	Large Wild Animals	Water Animals

MY CANADA

Kissing in the movies scandalous? At one time, most definitely! In 1895, May Irwin, a Whitby, Ontario actress, was the first to give a small peck to her co-star in a short film called – appropriately – The Kiss.

Name: _____

WEEK 31 — ACTIVITY 1 — TOTAL /5

Circle the *conjunction* in each sentence.

1. You need to keep working until the job is finished.

2. Halifax, which is the capital Nova Scotia, is an international seaport.

Correct these sentences.

3. shoting stars is also called meatiors sometimes thay hit the serfase of hour earth
   _____

4. in anshent times people beliefed that shoting stars meaned the gods was angry
   _____

Circle the prefix that means "together".

5. sub   post   co   inter

Name: _____

WEEK 31 — ACTIVITY 2 — TOTAL /5

Underline the *present participle* in each sentence.

1. The wind created a flurry of falling leaves.

2. "Oh, my aching head," said Davie.

Correct these sentences.

3. lighting ofen skips frum won clowd to another but not reely a problum
   _____

4. lighting jumping frum a clowd to the grownd can cawse serius damedge or injery
   _____

Complete the analogy.

5. V is to 5 as C is to _____

97

Name: _____

Underline the *independent clauses* in these sentences.

1. Even though I am not in the best shape, I am entering Saturday's race.

2. My sister is looking for a job now that she has graduated.

Circle the *subject* of this sentence.

3. When the painting is finished, clean out those brushes.   I / they / we / you

Correct these sentences.

4. jonah like to help hims grandpa plant rowse and rowse of corn in that there feeld
   _____

5. but the bestest part is builting a skare crow and dressing it in funny close
   _____

WEEK 31
ACTIVITY 3
TOTAL /5

Name: _____

Explain the underlined *idiom* in your own words.

1. I couldn't <u>keep a straight face</u> when I heard that story. _____

Correct these sentences.

2. moms book quik an eazy faily meels are soled in hour local bookstore the nook
   _____

3. sum of her bestest resipes appered in the magazeen working mom busy mom
   _____

Underline the predicate adjectives in each sentence.

4. An earthquake is dangerous and scary to people living in the area.

5. If an earthquake is severe and prolonged, damage can be extensive.

WEEK 31
ACTIVITY 4
TOTAL /5

Name: _____

Rewrite these sentences to correctly punctuate the dialogue.

1. Please whisper said the librarian so you don't disturb others

   _____

2. I'm almost finished my assignment I told Beth are you

   _____

3. Who can tell me asked Ms James the name of Ontario's Premier

   _____

4. Did you know that dog is dangerous asked Mac so don't pet him

   _____

5. A tractor is a farmer's most important machine explained Uncle Jed to Lee.

   _____

WEEK **31**

ACTIVITY **5**

TOTAL **/5**

Name: _____

Bonus Activity: Did You Really Mean What You Said?

The English language is full of expressions that cannot be taken literally. Imagine you are a person learning to speak English and you are hearing these expressions for the first time. **Illustrate your mental picture of each one.**

Jason's work is "head and shoulders" above the rest.	Slow down! Don't "put the cart before the horse".
She was "over the moon" when she heard she had won the prize.	I hope that deal you made is "above board".

WEEK **31**

MY CANADA — *Gordon Lightfoot's* song "The Wreck of the Edmund Fitzgerald" told the story of the sinking of the largest bulk ore carrier on the Great Lakes. In a severe storm on Nov. 10, 1975, 29 crew members lost their lives.

Name: _____

Correct these sentences.

1. the humin body are like a mashine it need care and manetinense like won too
   _____

2. humins can overcame dizease and injery if they lisen to theyre docters advise
   _____

Underline the future *perfect verb* in this sentence.

3. By the end of summer, Zara will have outgrown her basketball shoes.

***Subject pronoun* or *object pronoun*?**

4. <u>I</u> planted flowers seeds in the small peat pots. _____

5. When the seedlings are big enough, I will transplant <u>them</u>. _____

WEEK 32 — ACTIVITY 1 — TOTAL /5

Name: _____

Is this sentence *simple*, *compound*, or *complex*?

1. Whenever my dad has a day off work, it rains. _____

Correct these sentences.

2. plane yore campin trip carfully, colleckt them things you need yule be ready
   _____

3. george like to go fishin swimmin and hikeing i like to study plantes and inseckts
   _____

Underline the *conjunctions* in these sentences. Are they coordinating or subordinating?

4. Although I asked him to join us, he refused. _____

5. Either travel by car or by bus will be the quickest way to get there.
   _____

WEEK 32 — ACTIVITY 2 — TOTAL /5

Name: _____

Circle the word that best fits into each sentence.

1. Jeffrey is the boy _____ rescued the drowning puppy.   **who / that**

2. Johanna is very different _____ her sister Joelle.   **from / than**

Correct these sentences.

3. the top box compeny plan to build a knew factory hear in fallbrook nest yeer
_____

4. them manufacshure lite-wait storedge contaners of all sizes and shaps
_____

Circle the *indefinite pronouns* in this sentence.

5. Anybody and everybody can help with this project.

WEEK 32
ACTIVITY 3
TOTAL /5

Name: _____

Underline the *complete subject* and circle the *simple subject* in this sentence.

1. Newfoundland, one of our most beautiful provinces, joined Confederation in 1949.

Correct these sentences.

2. greta may you tell me wear you buyed that grate backpac i asked
_____

3. the store in the hampton mall have lottsa them in diffrent colors she replyed
_____

Underline the *infinitives* in each sentence.

4. To err is human, to forgive is divine.

5. Alfie wants to learn to ski and to skate better this winter.

WEEK 32
ACTIVITY 4
TOTAL /5

Name: _____

Combine these sentences into one good sentence.

1. The storm is turning into a blizzard. Tomorrow may be a "snow day" for us.
   _____

2. Brave explorers came to Canada. They faced many hardships. They made important discoveries.
   _____

3. Giles told me a secret. He told me not to tell anyone. I never will tell.
   _____

4. Maeve wants to be a vet. She loves animals. She is studying at university now.
   _____

5. Luke was hungry at breakfast. He ate two bowls of cereal. He ate three pieces of toast.
   _____

WEEK 32
ACTIVITY 5
TOTAL /5

Name: _____

Bonus Activity: A Not–So–Secret Message!

Discover the message by using the code below.

!	@	#	$	%	^	&	*	(	)	=	_	+	:	;	"	'	<	,	>	.	?	/	[	\	]
a	b	c	d	e	f	g	h	i	j	k	l	m	n	o	p	q	r	s	t	u	v	w	x	y	z

| ; | # | ! | : | ! | $ | ! | | ; | . | < | | * | ; | + | % | | ! | : | $ | | : | ! | > | (| ? | % | | = | ! | : | $ |

Using the code above, write your own short message. Have a friend decrypt it.

WEEK 32

MY CANADA Between 1948 and 2007, the average winter temperatures in the Yukon and northern British Columbia went up by 4.9° C. Can we really doubt that *global warming* is a fact?

ANSWER KEY

WEEK 1: ACTIVITY 1

1. Hey! Look at these! It's Canadian pennies which we no longer use.
2. Our coins are the loonie, toonie, quarter, dime, and nickel.
3. Rosi put her quarter <u>into</u> the (machine) but she didn't get a gumball.
4. A fierce wind blew the snow <u>over</u> the (highway.)
5. Our uncle <u>Paul is</u> coming to visit. Paul's

WEEK 1: ACTIVITY 2

1. The puppy <u>jumped</u> up on the bed, <u>grabbed</u> my library book and <u>began</u> to chew.
2. Eva was fascinated by the grace and poise of the ballerina in <u>The Nutcracker</u>.
3. She went to the evening performance at the Grand Theatre in Hamilton.
4. studios   5. nuclei

WEEK 1: ACTIVITY 3

1. octagon.   2. bed.
3. Their family has a big orchard with many varieties of apples.
4. They make delicious cider by chopping and pressing fresh apples.
5. Fragment

WEEK 1: ACTIVITY 4

1. We didn't leave our house <u>during</u> the (blizzard).
2. Mom got her car stuck in our (driveway).
3. We all agreed that Maxwell Downes is the most thoughtful boy in our class.
4. Mrs. Costini is opening a new flower shop called Blossom on Fourth Avenue.
5. Jake asked, "Does (anyone) know if we have math homework tonight?"

WEEK 1: ACTIVITY 5

1. September 24, 2015.
2. Dear Ms Greenlees:
3. I would like to invite you
4. ...next monthly meeting. Please...
5. Very truly yours,

BONUS ACTIVITY: WHAT HAPPENED NEXT?

Walking the Dog: 3, 5, 1, 2, 4
Cleaning Your Room: 2, 1, 4, 3, 5

WEEK 2: ACTIVITY 1

1. Last night Carrie forgot her ticket to the show and Lizzy forgot hers too.
2. Tokyo, the capital of Japan, is a huge city with millions of people.
3. The play <u>about</u> a talking dog entertained everyone <u>at</u> the assembly <u>on</u> Friday.
4. Workers are working <u>on</u> the roof <u>of</u> the house <u>next</u> door.
5. (The boys in my class) <u>are organizing a football team</u>.

WEEK 2: ACTIVITY 2

1. The glass of lemonade looked <u>cold, delicious</u> and <u>inviting</u>.
2. When my mother makes cookies, the kitchen (smells) like chocolate.
3. Modern life (has become) complicated for many people.
4. My cousins are very lucky to live on a ranch in Alberta.
5. We ate waffles with strawberries, syrup and whipped cream for breakfast.

WEEK 2: ACTIVITY 3

1. <u>A portrait of Sir John A. Macdonald</u> is on our $10 bill.
2. After he saw my phone bill Dad exclaimed, "We have to spend less money!"
3. On Tuesday we have to catch the 7:30 bus if we want to get to school early.
4. Intransitive   5. Transitive

WEEK 2: ACTIVITY 4

1. "We have less players on our team than they have on theirs," whined Davie.
2. There was an old, twisted, grapevine climbing the side of Eddy's barn.
3. Jackson, <u>who</u> is my cousin, will be the captain of our team.
4. Halifax, <u>which</u> is a big harbour, is the capital of Nova Scotia.
5. Imperative

WEEK 2: ACTIVITY 5

1. The waves <u>splashed</u> and <u>pounded</u> on the seawall.
2. The little child <u>took</u> a bath and <u>went</u> to bed.
3. The baby <u>smiled</u> and <u>laughed</u> at the teddy bear.
4. My dog <u>runs</u> and <u>jumps</u> and <u>plays</u> in the park.
5. The students <u>finished</u> their work and <u>corrected</u> it before the lunch break.

BONUS ACTIVITY: CONTEXT CLUES

1. most powerful, strongest, most plentiful   2. huge, enormous   3. simpler, less evolved, underdeveloped
4. no longer existing, disappeared

WEEK 3: ACTIVITY 1

1. Josh, Dylan, and Emmett forgot to tell their parents they needed a ride home.
2. Sally's aunt and uncle live in Ottawa and work on Parliament Hill.
3. Raw (carrots) are delicious and they are good for you.
4. (Joan of Arc) led troops into battle and she was victorious.
5. Transitive

WEEK 3: ACTIVITY 2

1. I always fall asleep under that warm, fuzzy blanket.
2. Ella got a bad burn from the hot handle of the pot.
3. When I graduate from high school, I plan to go to college.
4. Since you are a good student, I'm sure you'll have no problem.
5. When I returned to the classroom, Ms. Watson had already left.

WEEK 3: ACTIVITY 3

1. Sophie is the kindest friend that I have.
2. Little Ryan is noisier than his brother.
3. Although he searched all over for his books, he couldn't find any of them.
4. At the request of the principal, the students agreed to suggest ideas for fund raising.
5. I sent (Barbara) a postcard from Vancouver.

WEEK 3: ACTIVITY 4

1. When the cold weather arrives, I hunt for my mitts.
2. If you know where they are, please tell me.
3. Ruth was so hungry she ate four ham sandwiches for lunch.
4. Besides ham, she put lettuce, mustard, and pickles on each one.
5. Pauline Johnson is the poet who wrote "Prairie Greyhounds".

WEEK 3: ACTIVITY 5

1. capitalization error   2. spelling error   3. punctuation error   4. no error   5. capitalization error

BONUS ACTIVITY: IDIOMS

1. Dinner is free; someone else is paying for it.
2. Janie is very grumpy, cranky, cross.
3. I really don't know what is going on.
4. I spend all the money I have as soon as I get it.
5. He should make amends, set things right, apologize.
6. Callie didn't know how to do it.

WEEK 4: ACTIVITY 1

1. We are not ready to leave for school yet, but we will be once we eat breakfast.
2. At exactly 9:10 am, our bell rings to tell us class will begin.
3. Because we were shovelling gravel, we became dirty.
4. Nicky felt sick after riding the roller coaster.
5. Declarative

WEEK 4: ACTIVITY 2

1. ring is to finger as bracelet is to wrist
2. Black lab dogs are known for their intelligence and loyalty.   3. to make
4. The first kayaks were developed by ancestors of the Inuit many years ago.
5. They had a framework of whalebone or driftwood and were completely covered with seal skins.

WEEK 4: ACTIVITY 3

1. (Dean) burned his finger when he touched the hot dish.
2. The (company) will explain its proposal tomorrow.
3. My sister, Reba, is taking a trip to Simon Fraser University in British Columbia.
4. She wants to enrol in classes there for the upcoming semester.   5. precedent

WEEK 4: ACTIVITY 4

1. Intransitive   2. Transitive
3. Although Grandpa doesn't have any formal training, he can build almost anything.
4. He built a set of table and chairs for me and a high chair for my brother Stevie.
5. You've grown quite a bit.

WEEK 4: ACTIVITY 5

1. "I'll pick you up at three o'clock sharp," said Mom, "so be ready."
2. "That's fine with me," I replied. "I'll be waiting on the front step."
3. "Where are you going?" asked Jeff. "Can I go with you and Mom?"

4. "Not this time." I answered my little brother. "We are going to the dentist."
5. "You're right!" Jeff exclaimed. "I will go with you some other time."

BONUS ACTIVITY: OXYMORON

working vacation: you are on a holiday but still working
definite maybe: uncertain yes or no
1. icy hot   2. completely unfinished   3. jumbo shrimp
4. bitter sweet   5. exact estimate   6. forgettable memory

WEEK 5: ACTIVITY 1

1. almost: to what extent
2. "I am having trouble with some of those words," said George.
3. "Have you looked in the dictionary or thesaurus?" replied Ms. Bell.
4. After we wash the dishes, we will put them away.
5. We went into the movie just as it was starting.

WEEK 5: ACTIVITY 2

1. Whenever I hear that song, I want to dance.
2. We will help you as long as you co-operate with us.
3. Mom said, "Don't be late for dinner tonight because I have a meeting at the library."
4. They aren't going anywhere on the weekend because they have to work.
5. 5 mettle, 3 method, 1 meander, 2 medley, 4 metric

WEEK 5: ACTIVITY 3

1. The light was so bright it blinded (us).
2. They will pay (you) for all of your hard work.
3. Many (kinds) of birds can be found in that region of Canada.
4. The campfire cast dancing shadows on the people sitting nearby.
5. We are going to make a snack called S'mores from toasted marshmallows, wafers, and chocolate.

WEEK 5: ACTIVITY 4

1. Very quickly
2. The game of Trivia which is a lot of fun, is a Canadian invention.
3. You have to have a good memory and know a lot of information.
4. oats: plural   5. umiak: single

WEEK 5: ACTIVITY 5

1. Jack wanted to go camping with us but he got sick so he couldn't go.
2. When our sump pump stopped working, our basement flooded, making a huge mess.
3. Toronto, one of the biggest cities in Canada, used to be called York.
4. Although a small, white kitten that came to our door had no collar, we will try to find the owner.
5. Everyone was watching the final game of the World Series because it was exciting.

BONUS ACTIVITY: CONCRETE OR ABSTRACT?

A student in my class wrote a story about unusual courage. It told of a group of soldiers fighting in a foreign land. We value personal freedom in Canada and their bravery helped us to keep it. When they returned to their own country, they were honoured with a parade and presented with medals of valour. We should remain loyal to these citizens who fought to gain peace and freedom.

WEEK 6: ACTIVITY 1

1. My photos of our vacation turned out better than I expected.
2. Leo and Lena, my cousins, have invited us to go to the circus with them.
3. They have opened an animal rescue (centre) for abandoned (pets.)
4. They provide (food, shelter and medical care) for all the (animals.)
5. We did not have enough money for a treat, so we had to wait until another time

WEEK 6: ACTIVITY 2

1. accordingly: 4   pemmican: 3
2. We thought we heard something scratching on our window pane.
3. It was nothing more than a tree branch.
4. Carrots are a healthy vegetable that some people only eat raw.
5. I'm sure we'll see a lot of people we know at the anniversary party on Sunday.

WEEK 6: ACTIVITY 3

1. Wasn't out of danger
2. I hope to travel to Ireland to meet some of my relatives.
3. You need to feed the dog and to bath it.

4. In 1534, the King of France sent Jacques Cartier to North America.
5. His task was to search for gold and precious metals and then claim the land for France.

Week 6: Activity 4

1. Many settlers came over to Canada on crowded sailing ships.
2. Their journey was filled with dangers such as storms, lack of food, and disease.
3. You may either go to a movie or invite a friend over for dinner.
4. Not only is Darren a skillful athlete but he also is a good student.
5. Sharon hates getting to school after the bell rings.

Week 6: Activity 5

Thursday, December 6, 1917, was a bright clear day in Halifax, Nova Scotia. For some reason, two ships, the Mont Blanc, a munitions carrier, and the Norwegian steamer, Imo, steered for the same side of the narrow channel joining Halifax Harbour and Bedford Basin. When the ships collided, a fire ignited the munitions ship. The explosion blew the Mont Blanc to pieces and heaved the Imo onto the Dartmouth shore. On that disastrous day, 2000 people were killed and 9000 were injured. This became known as the Halifax Explosion.

Bonus Activity: Canadian, Eh?

Answers will vary.

Week 7: Activity 1

1. Those beautiful silver earrings were a gift from my grandmother Irene.
2. She wore them fifty years ago on her wedding day.
3. Neither Jill nor her sister are willing to help us.
4. Whether you believe me or not, that story is true.
5. Somebody left (you) a message.

Week 7: Activity 2

1. Do you think students should be forced to wear school uniforms?
2. Wouldn't it be expensive to buy them?
3. There has been a great deal of flooding in our community.
4. Sid the Kid is a nickname for NHL hockey player Sidney Crosby.
5. The most exciting time of my life was going to a One Direction rock concert.

Week 7: Activity 3

1. You
2. The girl swam across the pool and back at least eight times.
3. "My Grandpa Harry is kind, generous, and my best friend, " said Louis.
4. The (boy) played baseball with his friends.
5. (Marnie and Frank) rode their bikes to school.

Week 7: Activity 4

1. Fog covered the airport preventing several planes from landing.
2. "Did the magician pull a bouquet of flowers from under a scarf?" asked Billy.
3. Ghost is to Hallowe'en as bunny is to Easter.
4. Several kids in my math class are having trouble with the work.
5. A few of us are going to form a peer tutor group to help them.

Week 7: Activity 5

1. make him talk   2. tell information about his friends
3. dead   4. like a trapped animal   5. all alone

Bonus Activity: Tone

1. anxiety   2. sadness   3. excited   4. Joy, happiness
5. excitement

Week 8: Activity 1

1. Early explorers wondered if there really was a Northwest Passage around North America.
2. By 1845, most sailors knew that any passage would be locked in ice most of the year.
3. Simple   4. Complex
5. Mom's best qualities are her patience and her cheerfulness.

Week 8: Activity 2

1. You will pass the test if you have studied for it.
2. Hank tried to hit the target but missed every time.
3. penitentiary: 5
4. Jane works delivering pizza and she makes $25.00 every night.
5. Our school has a Junior Authors Club that I hope to join.

Week 8: Activity 3

1. Complete sentence   2. Fragment

3. Lynn and I are always arguing about who's the best soccer player.
4. If you really don't want a birthday present, I will donate to a charity.
5. Let's follow the path <u>into</u> the (field), <u>along</u> the (river) and <u>into</u> the (woods.)

Week 8: Activity 4

1. Reading is our favourite way to spend a rainy and cold afternoon.
2. If you don't want to read, we can play some board games.
3. (Brad) gave all the little kids a ride in <u>his</u> wagon.
4. I am returning this book <u>because</u> I have finished reading it.
5. You heard me calling you <u>yet</u> you did not answer me.

Week 8: Activity 5

1. We ate the delicious pancakes Mom cooked for breakfast.
2. Peter went to college in September to study to be a vet tech.
3. The car came to a halt when the battery went dead and now it will need to be towed.
4. I will gather the ingredients and read the directions before I start to make a cake.
5. Dad had a sore back from leaves all day Saturday so now he is going to the doctor.

Bonus Activity: Words! Words! Words!

Archaeologists worked for months in the <u>gloomy</u> (dark, damp) cave. They were trying to explain (decipher) the ancient code on the rock walls. The rough walls made it <u>difficult</u> (very hard) to see the markings. The carvings were barely <u>readable</u> (legible) even to the trained eye. Legend says some explorers had strangely <u>vanished</u> (disappeared) inside the cave. Sometimes <u>distinct/clear</u> (audible) moans could be heard in the distance. Do you believe such a thing is <u>real/genuine</u>? (true)

Week 9: Activity 1

1. Compound   2. Complex
3. Coffee, tea, and hot chocolate are served for breakfast in the diner.
4. My sister, Savannah, got a pair of fuzzy pyjamas for her birthday.
5. (The boy riding the bicycle) <u>is my brother</u>.

Week 9: Activity 2

1. (Because) they were so hungry, the boys gobbled their food.
2. We will be drawing names (and) buying gifts at Boys and Girls' Club.
3. I was late <u>for the bus</u>, so I grabbed an apple <u>for a snack</u> and a cookie <u>for a treat</u>.
4. A farmer living along the Niagara River in the 1700's sold a cow to an American farmer.
5. But the homesick cow swam back to her Canadian owner and would not live elsewhere.

Week 9: Activity 3

1. Transitive
2. During an electrical, storm the power may fail and be off for hours.
3. My oldest sister, Karen, was born on June 19, 2000, in Hamilton, Ontario.
4. How   5. When

Week 9: Activity 4

1. "Can you please give Tara some help loading the dishwasher?" asked Martha.
2. We love burgers and fries for our Friday night supper.
3. The locket I got for my birthday is <u>inscribed</u> with my initials. Engraved
4. This cake <u>smells</u> good and <u>tastes</u> even better!
5. The soccer player <u>was</u> a superstar but <u>appears</u> very shy.

Week 9: Activity 5

1. Punctuation   2. No error   3. Capitalization
4. Spelling   5. Punctuation

Bonus Activity: What's the Effect?

Answers will vary.

Week 10: Activity 1

1. The (crying) baby kept us awake all night.
2. The (howling) winds whipped the snow into big drifts.
3. Since they were sick, we couldn't watch the World Series together.
4. "Wipe your dirty boots before you come into my kitchen." said Aunt Lucy.
5. trans

Week 10: Activity 2

1. By the end of this week, <u>I will have finished</u> reading this book.
2. We <u>shall elect</u> a new leader of our student council.
3. <u>What</u> stores did you visit on your shopping trip?
4. The sun melted those icicles that were hanging from the roof.
5. Julie cut the watermelon into a dozen pieces for us to eat.

Week 10: Activity 3

1. Your story demonstrates <u>imagination</u> and <u>insight</u>.
2. Kelly's hobbies include the following: photography, sailing, and hiking.
3. He took a photo of an iceberg drifting off the shores of Labrador.
4. When we got to the theatre, <u>it was noisy and crowded</u>.
5. <u>Jack put his bike in the garage</u> so it wouldn't get wet in the rain.

Week 10: Activity 4

1. Colin was invited to a birthday party for his friend.
2. We went to the cafeteria to buy a turkey wrap for lunch.
3. "There isn't anything you can do about the weather!" exclaimed Grandpa.
4. "Can't anyone in our class solve this puzzle?" asked Fred.
5. Answers will vary.

Week 10: Activity 5

1. Sharon <u>who is a very kind person</u> tries to see the best in everyone. NR
2. Tarts are small pastry shells <u>that contain delicious fillings</u>. R
3. The Beech Bay Campground <u>where my family goes in summer</u> is nearby. NR
4. The sun <u>which was very hot today</u> gave me a sunburn. NR
5. The school <u>that I attended as a child</u> is closing in June. R

Bonus Activity: Idioms

1. fin   2. poem   3. cave   4. swim   5. Susan   6. Quebec

Week 11: Activity 1

1. Frannie's mom sewed every one of those costumes for our play.
2. It is a long long bus ride from Calgary to Ottawa.
3. <u>Anyone</u> can play this game and <u>nobody</u> will object.
4. <u>Somebody</u> left <u>something</u> on our front step today.
5. All students <u>in the band</u> will be going <u>to the competition in April</u>.

Week 11: Activity 2

1. mine   2. yours.
3. We are going on a vacation to Florida in the March break.
4. "Are you flying or driving your car?" asked Pete.
5. Fragment

Week 11: Activity 3

1. My favourite character in that story is the heroine, Princess Ella.
2. She was not afraid to defend her kingdom against the evil witch.
3. Soft <u>pattering</u> (rain) could be heard on the barn roof.
4. <u>Blowing</u> (snow) and <u>freezing</u> (rain) made driving dangerous.
5. The <u>game warden</u> will be checking for lawbreakers in that park. An officer who enforces laws that protect game and forests.

Week 11: Activity 4

1. Do we have any chocolate-covered raisins for my snack? interrogative
2. Help shovel the snow from the driveway and sweep off the steps. imperative
3. Whenever our dog, Jedi, sees the school bus, he jumps up and down in one spot.
4. I don't enjoy doing the dishes but I know that mom needs my help.
5. If you want <u>to succeed</u> you will need <u>to stay</u> focused and <u>to work</u> hard.

Week 11: Activity 5

1. Neither Bob nor I wanted to wash the car but Mom made us do it anyway.
2. We bought some fresh fruits and vegetables at the market.
3. My pen and pencil fell off my desk and onto the floor.
4. At the party Cory and Bill dressed up as ghosts and scared the little kids.
5. The cheerleaders and fans yelled loudly as they cheered for the home team.

Bonus Activity: Keep It Short

1. Junior   2. as soon as possible   3. August
4. maximum   5. etcetera   6. Bachelor of Arts
7. cash on delivery 8. Please reply (respondez s'il vous plait)   9. centimetre   10. continued

Week 12: Activity 1

1. Greg is <u>often</u> late, <u>seldom</u> prepared for class, and <u>frequently</u> tired.
2. Selma want to join the Mystery Readers Book Club but she is too busy right now.
3. We meet each Thursday at Lincoln Park Library at 4:00 pm sharp.
4. <u>Everyone</u> needs to find their uniform and return (it) to the coach.

5. He would never allow (it) to be lost.

Week 12: Activity 2

1. Vitamins found in fruits and vegetables are very good for your health.
2. We spent a lot of time practising our song for the concert.
3. The (girls) enjoyed that book so much that they read it twice.
4. Our dog barks at the (mailman) because it does not know him.   5. she'd   I'll

Week 12: Activity

1. "Watch out! Didn't you see that broken step?" asked Della.
2. "No, I didn't," Della replied. "Thanks for warning me."
3. Finish your report before it gets too late.
4. As soon as we heard the news, we all cheered.
5. reciprocal: 4   horizontal: 4

Week 12: Activity 4

1. If all goes well, Grandma Norma will arrive from Halifax on Sunday.
2. The book, Mystery of Skull Island is a real thriller so it might scare you.
3. masculine plural   4. feminine singular
5. Transitive

Week 12: Activity 5

1. Because Jimmy is learning to ride his bicycle, he needs to wear a helmet and pedal slowly.
2. Lucas and Tom love to play baseball so they play it every day.
3. When the movers came to our house to load our furniture, they were careful.
4. My computer is broken and will not turn on so I will need to get it repaired.
5. Alice wants a new Baby Susie doll for her birthday.

Bonus Activity: Time for Action!

This morning, I woke up late and jumped out of bed. I landed on my sister's stuffed dog, lost my balance, stumbled and fell. My sister Carrie came into my room, rubbed her eyes and demanded "Who is making all that noise?" I grumbled a few words and headed downstairs. Carrie walked slowly to her room and jumped back into bed. Mom heard the racket and came to see what was going on. "Why are you girls making so much noise on a Saturday morning?" she asked. "You woke up far too early." I nodded to show that I agreed with Mom, grabbed some toast and went back to my room so I could sleep some more.

Week 13: Activity 1

1. Until I hear from my sister, I will wait at home.
2. The whole class enjoyed the trip to the Royal Ontario Museum last March.
3. Everyone had their favourite exhibit but mine was animal habitats.
4. the maple tree's beautiful leaves
5. the final game's excited fans

Week 13: Activity 2

1. The music teacher taught the (choir) a new song.
2. A plant that resembles moss
3. Separated from; not keeping in touch
4. The fans were leaving because the game was dull and boring.
5. You shouldn't make plans for the weekend until you ask your parents.

Week 13: Activity 3

1. You will have the answer to your question soon. When
2. After a big snow is a great time to go tobogganing, skiing or ski-doing.
3. Wear warm clothes, thick mitts, your helmet, and remember to keep safe.
4. We noticed the inviting (smell) of popcorn as soon as we entered the theatre.
5. Blowing (snow) and lashing (winds) made driving difficult.

Week 13: Activity 4

1. Answers will vary.
2. Cora uses bright colours in her pictures but her sister, Hallie, prefers pastel colours.
3. "Are you looking for your reading glasses?" I asked Grandpa Ralph.
4. When (settlers) came to Canada, they had a difficult life.
5. The (country) was rich in resources but it was rugged and untamed.

Week 13: Activity 5

1. punctuation error   2. spelling error   3. capitalization error   4. punctuation error   5. capitalization error

BONUS ACTIVITY: ALL ABOUT ADJECTIVES

1. (old) man	old		old
2. (three) sisters		three	
3. (this) cookie			this
4. (yellow) socks	yellow		yellow
5. (those) flowers			those

WEEK 14: ACTIVITY 1

1. Linda showed Lara her new snowboard she got for Christmas.
2. The instructor offered to give her two free lessons during the break.
3. A legal claim on property for money owed
4. You want to make the basketball team <u>but</u> you don't come to practice.
5. We will rehearse every day <u>and</u> the play will be a success.

WEEK 14: ACTIVITY 2

1. In 1665, King Louis the XIV of France sent some mares and stallions to New France.
2. After a few years, every farmer in New France owned at least one horse of their own.
3. mine   4. his
5. Interrogative

WEEK 14: ACTIVITY 3

1. Charlie <u>was</u> telling a story about hunting bears with his uncle.
2. <u>Is</u> he making it up or could it be true?
3. "Will you drive me to baseball practice, Mom?" I asked politely.
4. "If you will help me do the dishes and clean up the kitchen," she replied.
5. The foreign (spy) risked his life to save his partner.

WEEK 14: ACTIVITY 4

1. When we got to the airport in Ottawa, the plane had already taken off.
2. We had to wait there for eight hours until the next flight was ready to take off.
3. Sam <u>had removed</u> his muddy shoes at the door.
4. Earlier that day, his mom <u>had placed</u> a mat at the door for him.
5. post

WEEK 14: ACTIVITY 5

1. The new owners have plans to renovate the old, rundown house.
2. No one noticed that the little boy was alone, cold and hungry.
3. When we went out for seafood dinner to Specialty Sea Foods, I had jumbo shrimp.
4. Have you seen Harry's painting showing a seascape of his grandparents' home?
5. Although Kent is very sick with strep throat, he didn't mention any signs of it and he didn't complain.

BONUS ACTIVITY: HOMOPHONES

1. might   2. hymn   3. cymbal   4. popular   5. franc
6. banned

WEEK 15: ACTIVITY 1

1. Besides being a soccer player, <u>Tony plays in the school band</u>.
2. <u>Andrea cleaned up her room</u> although she complained about it.
3. The old dog was lying <u>on the porch</u> <u>in the shade</u> of the <u>big oak tree</u>.
4. Since you will be late for school, I will give you a ride this once.
5. The fables and legends of a country tell a lot about its culture.

WEEK 15: ACTIVITY 2

1. (Greta), <u>who is my best friend</u>, visits her Grandma every Sunday.
2. We went fishing for trout all we caught was an old boot and a rusty can.
3. "Terry, shall I fry, boil, or oven roast your catch?" joked Dad.
4. mothers-in-law   5. avocados

WEEK 15: ACTIVITY 3

1. The task of raking all the leaves (seemed) impossible.
2. Do you have any honey doughnuts? Interrogative
3. What a close call we had on the road today! Exclamatory
4. Stella keeps a diary she writes in every day about things that have happened.
5. <u>The Last Voyage of the Scotian</u> is a exciting tale of adventure on a ship.

Week 15: Activity 4

1. Many people today live in (poverty) and (despair.)
2. Your (kindness) and (generosity) will not be forgotten.
3. Ross looked away from Mr. Markam's stern glance and began to work.
4. I am just starting to read The Dog that Wouldn't Be by Farley Mowat.
5. Passive

Week 15: Activity 5

1. Casey's favourite subjects in school are math, science, art, and sometimes history.
2. Tommy, could you play with the new boy at recess today?
3. Mrs. Bennett, would you like me to babysit after school tonight?
4. Amy wants to babysit, walk dogs, scoop ice cream, or deliver papers for the summer.
5. Melanie, you cannot borrow my bicycle ever again!

Bonus Activity   Story Board

Check to see if text and illustrations match.

Week 16: Activity 1

1. oriole: singular   lice: plural
2. The new calf wobbled on its (legs) and fell down to the (ground).
3. We found an old picture in a brass (frame) wrapped in an old (newspaper.)
4. John Franklin was an Arctic explorer who tried to find the Northwest Passage.
5. In 1845, his ships become trapped in the ice and his men were doomed to die.

Week 16: Activity 2

1. (Because) she is such a good player, every team wants her.
2. Intransitive   3. Transitive
4. That soup was cold but I ate it because I was so hungry.
5. Benny, who is my friend, helped me rake the leaves and put them in those bags.

Week 16: Activity 3

1. This (vase) is fragile because it is very old.
2. (Fannie) has a job so she is making her own money now.
3. (Not only) can Molly sing, (but also) she can dance.
4. Teddy read the return address on the envelope and opened it immediately.
5. Inside was an invitation to a birthday party at Cosmic World Extreme Games.

Week 16: Activity 4

1. I have a new mountain bike so I want to join the Big Bike Cycling Club.
2. The Rocky Mountains stretch across British Columbia and Alberta.
3. Glittering jewels and golden objects (filled) the treasure chest.
4. Mrs. Rogers (teaches) Celeste piano lessons.
5. responsibility: 6   Athabasca: 4

Week 16: Activity 5

1. Compound   2. Simple   3. Compound   4. Complex
5. Complex

Bonus Activity: Up North Word Search

i	n	u	k	s	h	u	k				d
n				s	g	r	e	b	e	c	i	o
u		c			e							g
i		a		i		e	e	g	c	m	m	a	s
t		r		k	c				x			l
		i		s		e		o				e
		b		u			f					d
	n	o	r	t	h	e	r	n	l	i	g	h	t	s
		u							o			
		r	a	e	b	r	a	l	o	p	e	

Week 17: Activity 1

1. The first inhabitants of Canada came from Asia thousands of years ago.
2. Early explorers called them Indians but today we call them native people.
3. They were very hot and thirsty after the game.
4. The sunset glowed red, orange and pink.
5. Intransitive

Week 17: Activity 2

1. Jenny received a card in the mail from her uncle in Dartmouth.
2. For the last time, put the cover on the pot and set it on the stove.
3. The beautiful province of British Columbia is known for tall forests and tall mountains.
4. Because we were cooking, mom opened the windows to get some fresh air.

5. A stitch in time saves nine. Looking after a small problem right away saves work later on.

Week 17: Activity 3

1. We sent everyone in our family party (invitations) for Mom's birthday.
2. The babysitter made the children a good (supper) last night.
3. improperly
4. My little cousin, Abby, sings "Teddy Bears Picnic" while she is playing.
5. She has a whole collection of stuffed bears that she has named.

Week 17: Activity 4

1. Lieut.   2. Esq.
3. We're having a bake sale to raise money for new instruments for our school band.
4. Lee is the most talented musician in Fieldrow High's band.
5. Ping Pong is to paddle as tennis is to racquet.

Week 17: Activity 5

1. Are you coming with us out for dinner now?
2. Luke has a cold and can't play in tonight's game so Don will have to play for him.
3. Cacti are hardy plants that don't require much water so they are the best plants for me.
4. Move the cake, quick, before the ants crawling on the picnic table reach it.
5. I couldn't stop my dog when he ran away, right through the neighbour's flower bed.

Bonus Activity: Palindromes

1. mom   2. sis   3. eye   4. noon   5. peep   6. gag
7. did   8. toot

Week 18: Activity 1

1. Fragment   2. Complete sentence
3. Michael wanted to buy new pair of running shoes but they were too expensive.
4. That old letter in my grandma's trunk is dated May 21, 1874.
5. We were thinking of you when you called.

Week 18: Activity 2

1. February will bring us more (snow.)
2. Did she tell you her (secret)?
3. "Your project on the Avro Arrow was excellent," Ms. Herman told Lila.
4. She worries about everything whether she has a reason to or not.
5. anniversary

Week 18: Activity 3

1. Surfers like to stand on their boards and ride high on the waves.
2. The scared little boy clung to his mother's legs and wouldn't go into the school.
3. (She) told us all about her shopping trip to the mall.
4. I don't like hornets. (One) stung me yesterday on my arm.
5. Our town has an active, volunteer fire department.

Week 18: Activity 4

1. Apply some sunscreen before going to the beach. you
2. On a hot humid day, you should stay in the shade and drink a lot of water.
3. Marty thought he heard a strange sound behind that old shed.
4. who   5. which

Week 18: Activity 5

1. Simple subject: brother   Simple predicate: made
2. Simple subject: we   Simple predicate: bought
3. Simple subject: bear   Simple predicate: lumbered
4. Simple subject: children   Simple predicate: avoid
5. Simple subject: protesters   Simple predicate: marched

Bonus Activity: Context Clues

1. A beginner; someone new at doing something
2. Something dishonest; a trick
3. Abide by; follow; stick to
4. Became less or smaller
5. Scolded harshly

Week 19: Activity 1

1. Yesterday we saw Ron and Serena at our neighbourhood pool with their parents.
2. The Andes mountains run all the way down the coast of South America.
3. When our friends are in trouble, we try to help out.
4. mine   5. hers

Week 19: Activity 2

1. Mario played a good game even though he had a bad headache most of the time.

2. All that construction makes it very noisy in my neighbourhood
3. "Kenneth, where in the world did you put the keys to my workshop?" asked Dad.
4. We like watching TV and playing games on the weekend.
5. Reading and writing are important skills to learn.

Week 19: Activity 3

1. Whether you go with us or stay home, you must decide soon.
2. The sky grew darker and darker by the minute.
3. It became evident that we were getting a thunderstorm soon.
4. The first colony in Canada was established by the French on the Bay of Fundy.
5. The colony was called Acadia and the first settlement there was called Port Royal.

Week 19: Activity 4

1. Declarative   2. Interrogative
3. Unless we start to work faster, we won't finish this job on time.
4. Sharon looked in disgust at the mess that her brothers had made in the living room.
5. Potato chip crumbs, pizza crusts, empty pop cans and plates were everywhere.

Week 19: Activity 5

1. less   2. many / most   3. better   4. bad / worst
5. some / most

Bonus Activity: Idioms

1. Don't be overly confident
2. Trying to fool me
3. Most delicious ever tasted
4. We share the same situation
5. Reprimanded, scolded

Week 20: Activity 1

1. (Rob and Lori) love their new pet puppy
2. I received your message late and could not answer. when
3. Mr. Bronson was quite happy with my performance in the play. To what extent
4. The boy wanted a cap similar to the one he had lost.
5. It has the name of his favourite baseball team, the Toronto Blue Jays

Week 20: Activity 2

1. The original Johnny Canuck appeared in newspaper cartoons in the 1880s.
2. The tall tale hero dressed as a lumberjack, a farmer, and sometimes as a rancher,
3. The windows that face the east will let in the most sunshine.
4. The lake where we caught all the fish is our secret.
5. Pat, who is my neighbour, walks her dog four times a day.

Week 20: Activity 3

1. Although I believe your story, others may not.
2. My cousin, Kenton B. Thomas, is a reporter for the Vancouver Sun.
3. Once he let me go with him to interview a famous mystery writer.
4. Many of the children would like to go to summer camp.
5. The supervisor will speak to anyone who is interested.

Week 20: Activity 4

1. (We) will pick them up after school today.
2. (They) hit us with snowballs when we weren't looking.
3. We are reading a good book in our English class with Mr. Hudson.
4. It is called Underground to Canada which is the story of Harriet Tubman.
5. The wind grabbed the papers from my hand.

Week 20: Activity 5

1. "Mom, I'm home from school," Theo called. "Can I have a snack?"
2. "Let's watch this program," Reagan suggested. "It's called The History of Rock and Roll."
3. The principal began, "Today we have a serious matter to discuss with all of you."
4. "Will you be here when Gwen's parents arrive?" inquired her Aunt Sadie.
5. "I want to tell you about my hobby," Artie said. "I collect old comic books."

Bonus Activity: A is for ...

6 absurd, 19 argument, 11 ahoy
3 abide, 17 applicant, 2 abandon
10 agility, 1 abacus, 14 amiable
20 athlete, 4 abnormal, 13 alert
8 aerial, 5 about-face, 18 appreciate
15 ancient, 22 awesome, 19 affirm
16 antagonist, 23 axe, 24 azure
7 accident, 12 airsick, 21 auditory

Week 21: Activity 1

1. (Marion) is good company because <u>she</u> is so funny.
2. My (dad), who has started a new job, has <u>his</u> office in downtown Winnipeg.
3. Because of the blizzard, we missed playing our rival team, the Falcons.
4. "Do you think we had a chance of beating them?" asked Perry.
5. We are all ready <u>so</u> let's go outside.

Week 21: Activity 2

1. William's family moved to Swift Current, Saskatchewan, on June 29, 2013.
2. Do you smell that delicious odour?" asked Jon. "Someone is barbecuing burgers!"
3. Good <u>manners</u> will always be valued and respected.
4. Peter's <u>charm</u> and good <u>humour</u> have made him popular.
5. Complex

Week 21: Activity 3

1. stormier / stormiest
2. "I have just finished reading a book called <u>Secrets of the Frozen Seas</u>," said Mark.
3. It told of brave explorers trying to travel across the icy lands of Canada's Arctic.
4. I <u>don't have any</u> time.
5. He <u>doesn't have anywhere</u> to go.

Week 21: Activity 4

1. Ed needs to get a job and save a lot of money to go on the student exchange.
2. His class wants to pair up with a school in Moosonee, Ontario.
3. Simple   4. Compound
5. harder

Week 21: Activity 5

1. Last night, during the bad thunder and lightning storm, our pets were afraid.
2. I can't meet you at noon today because I have a job interview but I will see you later.
3. When the horses reached the cool stream, they stopped to drink because they were hot and thirsty.
4. Lois hasn't phoned or texted us for two weeks so we are worried about her.

Bonus Activity: Animal Idioms

1. my stomach was upset
2. is he crazy, not being realistic
3. to say mean things; gossip

Week 22: Activity 1

1. I did not dare <u>to speak</u> while dad was scolding me.
2. Several people stepped forward <u>to help</u> the stranger.
3. Miramichi: 4
4. The short, quiet boy stood by the fence, watching the boys play soccer.
5. Joelle is working harder than ever to make the cheerleading team.

Week 22: Activity 2

1. After the play <u>ended</u>, the audience <u>clapped</u>. Simple past
2. <u>When the oven is hot enough</u>, put in the casserole.
3. Jaxon left <u>before I had a chance to ask him about our homework</u>.
4. Gram said, "Life was harder years ago, but we had a lot of family fun."
5. "We even managed to get along without a telephone or television," she chuckled.

Week 22: Activity 3

1. <u>While we were on vacation</u>, we made many new friends.
2. I will help him with his math <u>because</u> he asked me.
3. haberdasher / lamination
4. The Belcher Islands, located in Hudson Bay, belongs to Nunavut.
5. Next week, oour class are reading Shakespeare's play <u>Romeo and Juliet</u>.

Week 22: Activity 4

1. My kitten seems ill because it won't even drink water.
2. Jane, who is my best friend, was elected president of the Student Council.
3. Everybody who knows her was surprised when she quit the basketball team.
4. Those brownies are <u>sweet</u>, <u>chocolatey</u>, and <u>delicious</u>.
5. The children seem <u>happy</u> and <u>contented</u> in their new home.

Week 22: Activity 5

John Cabot, an Italian explorer, may have landed on the shores of Newfoundland or Nova Scotia. He claimed the land for King Henry of England and began his journey home. His ship, the Matthew, crossed over the Grand Banks and came upon great schools of cod fish. The crew wanted to catch some to provide a food supply for the long voyage. At first their methods proved unsuccessful. Then one sailor suggested, "Let us try baskets." The idea worked and the crew were rewarded with tons of gleaming fish.

BONUS ACTIVITY: WHAT'S NEXT?

Answers will vary.

WEEK 23: ACTIVITY 1

1. When all that snow fell, the path to the street became invisible.
2. The bay was choppy and dangerous as the fishing boats prepared to set out.
3. A cowboy on a horse appeared on the horizon.
4. The mother (dog) bunched up a blanket to cover her newborn puppies.
5. (Jade) sent a gift to her cousin in Edmonton.

WEEK 23: ACTIVITY 2

1. Did you notice those fans sitting near us wearing Ottawa Senators jerseys?
2. When I get my pay cheque, I'll put some money in the bank and spend some on treats.
3. Many people live in large cities.
4. Our kitchen is our family meeting place.
5. non

WEEK 23 ACTIVITY 3:

1. The crowd screamed, " Go, Kyle, Go!" as he rushed toward the net with the ball.
2. The lead singer of the all-girl band, Street Angels, sang my favourite song.
3. It takes a lot of energy and determination to succeed in sports.
4. His dog, Duke, is faithful and loyal.
5. The clouds looked dark and ominous.

WEEK 23: ACTIVITY 4

1. kilogram / telegram
2. Transitive   3. Intransitive
4. British Columbia is the western-most province in Canada.
5. British Columbia has a warmer climate which makes it a popular place to live.

WEEK 23: ACTIVITY 5

1. Simple subject: uncle   Simple predicate: constructed
2. Pronoun: its   Antecedent: construction
3. Direct object: care   Indirect object: plants
4. Complete subject: Our whole family
   Simple predicate: helps

5. Preposition: in   Object of a preposition: greenhouse

BONUS ACTIVITY: HOMOPHONES CROSSWORD

m	e	a	t			s	t	e	a	l
			o				t			
			w		t	a	l	e		
			e			r			f	
		m	e	d	d	l	e		p	l
w	e	a	k					w	o	o	d
		n							u	u
	h	e	a	r					r	r

WEEK 24: ACTIVITY 1

1. hers
2. My dad's army photo shows him standing among his fellow soldiers at CFB Kingston.
3. Although I like that new band, I probably wouldn't buy their current CD, Look at This.
4. Time marches on and waits for no one.
5. Our hedge was standing knee deep in snow.

WEEK 24: ACTIVITY 2

1. The buffet table was loaded with good things to eat. Simple
2. Roast chicken, salad, and fresh buns caught my eye. Compound
3. I have a friend, John, living down the street, who is in my class.
4. Last night the sky was cloudless, so the Big Dipper stood out quite plainly.
5. Quickly, yet stealthily, Joanne hid the present that she bought yesterday.

WEEK 24: ACTIVITY 3

1. oases
2. This year's basketball championship tournament is being held at Redford High.
3. Gary and I watched an interesting show on Nat Geo Wild called Under the Ice Cap.
4. Harry, close the door, please.
5. The spring months are March, April, and May.

WEEK 24: ACTIVITY 4

1. As the storm approached, the animals took shelter

under the big oak trees.
2. A blanket of fresh snow lay deep on the roof of vacant old house.
3. He ran across the road, through the barnyard, and into the stable.
4. We sat in front of the open fire, watching the dance of the flames.
5. Imperative

WEEK 24: ACTIVITY 5

1. Heavy clouds hid the sun. Active.
   The sun was hidden by the clouds. Passive
2. The house was struck by lightning. Passive
   Lightning struck the house. Active
3. The teacher gave Caleb the prize. Active
   Caleb was given the prize by the teacher. Passive
4. Aunt Cassie sent me a birthday present. Active
   My birthday present was sent by Aunt Cassie. Passive
5. He was seen leaving the theatre by two people. Passive
   Two people saw him leave the theatre. Active

BONUS ACTIVITY: IT'S ALL ABOUT FOOD

Where We Keep Food	Places to Eat Food	What We Do to Food	Items to Help Us Cook
cupboard	kitchen	freeze	stove
bag	drive-through	nibble	pot
freezer	canteen	chew	microwave oven
box	cafeteria	roast	frying pan
refrigerator	picnic table	prepare	toaster
jar	restaurant	broil	barbeque

WEEK 25: ACTIVITY 1

1. In history class today, we learned about Amelia Earhart, a courageous pilot.
2. As the first woman to fly over the Atlantic Ocean, she was admired by many people.
3. Sarah covered her eyes while we were watching the monster movie.
4. After it was over, she declared she was never afraid.
5. Pete and Hallie went to the amusement park and rode on the roller coaster.

WEEK 25: ACTIVITY 2

1. Isn't the Davidson's new house in that subdivision on Monarch Drive?
2. "Yes, I think you are correct," replied Harrison. "They moved there last Saturday."
3. The audience clapped when the choir finished the final performance.

4. Mt. Nesselrode: 4   5. Matagami: 4

WEEK 25: ACTIVITY 3

1. Willy is telling a different story than you are telling.
2. We are leaving right now so get ready please.
3. The top speed on that highway is 100 kilometres per hour.
4. If you exceed that limit. you will be fined and maybe lose points on your licence.
5. my parents' surprise party

WEEK 25: ACTIVITY 4

1. Even though Mom's car is newer than Dad's, hers has the highest number of kilometres.
2. Flour, eggs, vinegar, and shortening are used in this pie crust recipe.
3. perfect
4. I need to sharpen my skates before I can go skating with you.
5. As soon as he realized they were missing, Jared starting looking for his keys.

WEEK 25: ACTIVITY 5

1. Johnny Brown, a rookie on our hockey team, is a great asset to the game.
2. My favourite exercise, playing on a soccer team, helps keep me in shape.
3. Jace's ultimate goal, to go to medical school, is the reason he works so hard.
4. My uncle, a longtime world traveller, has many exciting tales to tell our family.
5. Their journey, starting out as a short one, soon became more and more lengthy.

BONUS ACTIVITY: STEVE NASH

1. F   2. T   3. F

WEEK 26: ACTIVITY 1

1. Take responsibility, accept punishment
2. Makes things worse
3. "Where did you learn to play the piano so well?" asked Freddy.
4. Commercial jets are seldom struck by lightning but turbulence is a problem.
5. That new grocery (store) is very clean and its produce selection is excellent.

WEEK 26: ACTIVITY 2

1. Anita, who is my best friend, is moving away in August.

2. Provincial parks, that are owned by the government, are great to visit.
3. Metaphor
4. Nanook of the North, a silent movie, was about a group of Inuit living along Hudson Bay.
5. Made in 1922, it was recognized as the first full-length documentary film.

WEEK 26: ACTIVITY 3

1. After three attempts to climb the mountain, Kelly gave up.
2. I love soup for lunch, especially if it is homemade.
3. I always have to read The Three Little Pigs to my cousin when I babysit him.
4. June 22, 2016, will be graduation day for my classmates and me.
5. Future

WEEK 26: ACTIVITY 4

1. Casey at the Bat, written by Ernest L. Thayer, is a funny poem about a baseball player.
2. It shows us what can happen when a person is too arrogant and has foolish pride.
3. This is the (bad) worst storm we have had this winter.
4. I love chocolate cake! It's the (good) best !
5. My dreams for the future (involve) travel and making new friends.

WEEK 26: ACTIVITY 5

1. Please note that this cheque is for one hundred (100) dollars.
2. There is new research available on the West Nile virus from the WHO (World Health Organization).
3. My cousin Barb (who is also my best friend) is teaching me to play the clarinet.
4. Originally there were only six teams in the NHL (National Hockey League).
5. Sir. John A. Macdonald (1815 – 1891) was a colourful character in our history.

BONUS ACTIVITY: EXTRA! EXTRA!

Answers will vary.

WEEK 27: ACTIVITY 1

1. Strawberries are my favourite kind of fruit so I eat a lot of them when they're in season.
2. My friend, Marla, lives on the fourth floor of the building right next to the J. H. Newton Library.
3. Pug puppies are so friendly, adorable and loving.
4. The mother bear was fearless and relentless in her fight to protect her cub.
5. Interrogative

WEEK 27: ACTIVITY 2

1. Chris told (his friends) all about his vacation plans.
2. I tossed my little (cousin) the ball as gently as I could.
3. 3 confront, 1 concave, 2 condemn, 5 convey, 4 contrast, 6 convince
4. Famous country western singers appear at the Calgary Stampede each year.
5. Because she moved to New Brunswick in Grade 3, Cheryl speaks French really well.

WEEK 27: ACTIVITY 3

1. Cranky, whiny
2. Rude, coarse, low class
3. "Look this way, smile, and don't blink," the photographer said to our class.
4. All those TV networks are carrying the story of the brave rescue by the Ski Patrol.
5. sub

WEEK 27: ACTIVITY 4

1. Sad, upset, depressed
2. The Junior Players Troop is performing a play called To Be a Child on Sunday.
3. The final scene will be performed by the entire cast while they are all on stage at once.
4. Complex   5. Compound

WEEK 27: ACTIVITY 5

1. January 27, 2016   2. Dear Ms Radford   3. Thank
4. Family Literacy Day   5. Yours truly,

BONUS ACTIVITY: ISLANDS

V	A	N	C	O	U	V	E	C	R		E
B	I		B	A	N	K	S	T			R
E	N	C				S					E
L	E		T		O				B	M	
C	L			O	C				A	S	
H	A			I	R				F	E	
E	D		T			I			F	L	
R	G	N				A			I	L	
M	A	N	I	T	O	U	L	I	N	N	E
	M		I	K	S	I	M	I	K	A	

Week 28: Activity 1

1. <u>Swimming</u> and <u>diving</u> are Theo's best sports.
2. <u>Waiting</u> for us to get ready was making Mom impatient.
3. Those soccer cleats look really good but they're too expensive for me to buy.
4. "Why don't you use some of your birthday money?" asked Victor.
5. Buffalo Narrows: 5   Ungava Peninsula: 7

Week 28: Activity 2

1. Lily said <u>she'd</u> help me finish the posters for the bake sale.
2. "Quinn, do you want to go to the Boys and Girls Club tonight?" asked Wanda.
3. They are going to teach us a new dance and show us how to cook lasagna.
4. That poor stray dog looks mangy, underfed and <u>unwell</u>.
5. Spring weather is <u>warm</u>, <u>fresh</u> and <u>inviting</u>.

Week 28: Activity 3

1. A cruise <u>from</u> (Vancouver) <u>to</u> (Alaska) is one <u>of the most beautiful</u> (trips.)
2. Laws are made <u>by the</u> (people) and <u>for the</u> (good) <u>of the</u> (people).
3. Remember Elton is <u>innocent</u> until proven <u>guilty</u>.
4. Randall is an intelligent boy but sometimes he can be very rude to others.
5. Sugar, fruit and nuts give flavour to ice cream while eggs and gelatin make it smooth.

Week 28: Activity 4

1. halves   sheep
2. "What a day of wild weather! We had snow wind and freezing rain ," remarked Yanni.
3. Many people love winter sports: skiing, snowshoeing, skating and ice fishing.
4. M   5. N

Week 28: Activity 5

1. British Columbia, the western-most Canadian province, borders on the Pacific Ocean.
2. About 200 years ago, Captain Cook landed on Vancouver island where he traded goods for furs with the native people.
3. People work in many industries: sawmills, wood factories, fish canneries, and jobs in the vast forests.
4. British Columbia is extremely mountainous because the Rocky Mountains run through the province, creating beautiful scenery.

Bonus Activity: Drink Up!

1. F   2. T   3. F

Week 29: Activity 1

1. Mr. Keyes explanation of the combustion engine was clear and concise .
2. Ingrid and Olive (who are Patty's best friends) said they would be glad to help out.
3. Lighthouses have <u>sent</u> (send) out signals to ships to guide them.
4. Lighthouses have <u>kept</u> (keep) ships out of danger.
5. I never talk to Mom <u>until she has had her first cup of coffee</u>.

Week 29: Activity 2

1. The jury couldn't reach a unanimous decision so it was a "hung jury".
2. Anaka studied piano with Ms. Dreyfus for six years and her hard work has paid off.
3. A reminder, a keepsake   4. Very dangerous, unsafe
5. Synonyms

Week 29: Activity 3

1. Robins, blue jays, chickadees, and sparrows all visit Grandpa's bird feeders.
2. "Who's the generous person that sent me these movie tickets?" I whispered.
3. The thunder <u>appeared</u> to be a warning of the coming storm.
4. The windshield <u>looked</u> like frosted glass.
5. Fragment

Week 29: Activity 4

1. My grandparents are amazed by the (progress) in everyday (technology.)
2. They built their house on high (ground) in a sheltered (area).
3. The Bayview Community Hall was built in August, 2009, near our school.
4. Often Aunt Dolly likes to sit on her front porch and read her sewing magazines.
5. <u>Oh great</u>! Now I have to babysit my baby brother!

Week 29: Activity 5

1. "Come again," said Petra, "when you can stay longer and visit."
2. "Hey!" Larry shouted. "Wait for me. I'll be right there."
3. " I didn't mean to lose your bracelet," I said to my sister. "Will you forgive me?"
4. "Try this flavour of ice cream," suggested Connie. "It's called spumoni."
5. "I hope you are hungry," said Dad, "because I am in the mood to barbeque."

Bonus Activity: Where Do I Look?

1. atlas   2. encyclopedia   3. thesaurus, dictionary
4. dictionary   5. thesaurus, dictionary   6. cookbook

Week 30: Activity 1

1. excitement   appearance
2. Our neighbour, Mr. Benson, has the biggest and best garden on our street.
3. It's his hobby so he gives much of his harvest to his lucky neighbours.
4. When the towels were dry, we removed them from the clothes dryer.
5. The Lunch Box serves its meals faster than other places.

Week 30: Activity 2

1. Transitive
2. "Eddie is my nickname," the girl explained, "but my real name is Edwina."
3. His friends always tease Nick about his red hair but he just laughs.
4. hers   5. his

Week 30: Activity 3

1. We all have new scarves and hats. Mine are red and my brothers are blue.
2. Zoe and Kara are going hiking next weekend together.
3. There is no substitute for intelligence, enthusiasm, and honesty.
4. Imperative   5. Declarative

Week 30: Activity 4

1. "It's not fair," said Jerome, "that I have to miss the best movie of the year."
2. If you're hungry, have a light snack so you don't spoil your dinner.
3. like   4. slowest   5. quicker

Week 30: Activity 5

1. If you like chicken soup better than tomato, then have the kind you prefer.
2. It's a shame you dog doesn't like its new collar.
3. Leave their mail over there on the table.
4. Whose jacket is this and who's going to return it?
5. We are all ready to leave and you have spilled something on your shirt already.

Bonus Activity: Animals Everywhere

Farm Animals: boar; stallion; heifer; kid; foal; ewe
Small Wild Animals: hare; weasel; badger; pika; gopher; marmot
Large Wild Animals: wolverine; caribou; buffalo; reindeer; grizzly bear; muskox
Water Animals: newt; polliwog; whale; walrus; lobster; seal

Week 31: Activity 1

1. You need to keep working (until) the job is finished.
2. Halifax, (which) is the capital Nova Scotia, is an international seaport.
3. Shooting stars (also called meteors) sometimes hit the surface of our earth.
4. In ancient times, people believed that shooting stars meant the gods were angry.
5. co

Week 31: Activity 2

1. The wind created a flurry of falling leaves.
2. "Oh, my aching head," said Davie.
3. Lightning often skips from one cloud to another but that's not really a problem.
4. Lightning jumping from a cloud to the ground can cause serious damage or injury.
5. V is to 5 as C is to 100

Week 31: Activity 3

1. Even though I am not in the best shape, I am entering Saturday's race.
2. My sister is looking for a job now that she has graduated.
3. you
4. Jonah likes to help his grandpa plant rows and rows of corn in that field.
5. But the best part is building a scarecrow and dressing it in funny clothes.

Week 31: Activity 4

1. Couldn't hide my expression; had to smile
2. Mom's book, <u>Quick and Easy Family Meals</u>, is sold in our local bookstore, The Nook.
3. Some of her best recipes appeared in the magazine <u>Working Mom, Busy Mom</u>.
4. An earthquake is <u>dangerous</u> and <u>scary</u> to people living in the area.
5. If an earthquake is <u>severe</u> and <u>prolonged</u>, damage can be <u>extensive</u>.

Week 31: Activity 5

1. "Please whisper," said the librarian, "so you don't disturb others."
2. "I'm almost finished my assignment," I told Beth. "Are you?"
3. "Who can tell me," asked Ms James, "the name of Ontario's Premier?"
4. "Did you know that dog is dangerous?" asked Mac. "So don't pet him."
5. "A tractor is a farmer's most important machine," explained Uncle Jed to Lee.

Bonus Activity: Did You Really Mean What You Said?

Jason's work is "head and shoulders" above the rest.	Slow down! Don't "put the cart before the horse".
She was "over the moon" when she heard she had won the prize.	I hope that deal you made is "above board".

Week 32: Activity 1

1. The human body is like a machine because it needs care and maintenance like one.
2. Humans can overcome disease and injury if they listen to their doctor's advice.
3. By the end of summer, Zara <u>will have outgrown</u> her basketball shoes.
4. Subject pronoun   5. Object pronoun

Week 32: Activity 2

1. Complex
2. Plan your camping trip carefully and collect the things you need so you'll be ready.
3. George likes to go fishing, swimming, and hiking while I like to study plants and insects.
4. <u>Although</u> I asked him to join us, he refused. Subordinating
5. <u>Either</u> travel by car <u>or</u> by bus will be the quickest way to get there. Coordinating

Week 32: Activity 3

1. who   2. from
3. The Top Box Company plans to build a new factory here in Fallbrook next year.
4. They manufacture light-weight storage containers of all sizes and shapes.
5. (Anybody) and (everybody) can help with this project.

Week 32: Activity 4

1. <u>(Newfoundland), one of our most beautiful provinces,</u> joined Confederation in 1949.
2. "Greta, will you tell me where you bought that great backpack?" I asked.
3. "The store in the Hampton Mall has a lot of them in different colours," she replied.
4. <u>To err</u> is human, <u>to forgive</u> is divine.
5. Alfie wants to learn <u>to ski</u> and <u>to skate</u> better this winter.

Week 32: Activity 5

1. The storm is turning into a blizzard so tomorrow may be a "snow day" for us.
2. Brave explorers coming to Canada faced many hardships but they still made important discoveries.
3. When Giles told me a secret, he told me not to tell anyone and I never will.
4. Because she loves animals, Maeve wants to be a vet so she is studying at university now.
5. Luke was so hungry at breakfast that he ate two bowls of cereal and three pieces of toast.

Bonus Activity: A Not – So – Secret Message!

OCanada Our home and native land

www.ingramcontent.com/pod-product-compliance
Lightning Source LLC
Chambersburg PA
CBHW081204240426
43669CB00039B/2802